ISSUE 9

THE
POINT

WINTER 2015

WWW.THEPOINTMAG.COM

TABLE *of* CONTENTS

essays

symposium: what is privacy for?

reviews

THE POINT

THE EDITORS	Jon Baskin
	Jonny Thakkar
	Etay Zwick
MANAGING EDITOR	Rachel Wiseman
DESIGN	Marie Otsuka
	Etay Zwick
COVER ART	*Human Ear*, from the Museum of Science & Industry, 1950-1960, The Jordan L. Smith Collection
ART EDITOR	Claire Rabkin
INTERNS	Daniel Moattar
	Christopher Siegler
ASSOCIATE EDITOR	Evan Weiss
EDITORIAL CONSULTANT	Gregory Freeman
COPY EDITORS	Lindsay Knight
	John Colin Bradley
EDITORIAL BOARD	Danielle Allen
	Thomas Bartscherer
	J. C. Gabel
	Jonathan Lear
	Mark Lilla
	Martha Nussbaum
	Geof Oppenheimer
	Robert Pippin
	Douglas Seibold
	Tom Stern
	Ralph Ubl
ADDRESS	2 N. La Salle St., #2300
	Chicago, IL 60602
DISTRIBUTION	Harry Backlund

The Point is based in Chicago and published twice a year. Subscribe at *www.thepointmag.com* or correspond with us at info@thepointmag.com. *The Point* is grateful for the support of the Helen Zell Foundation, the Orphiflamme Foundation, Sheldon Baskin and our Kickstarter donors. *The Point*, no. 9 © 2014 *The Point* Magazine. ISSN: 2153-4438. ISBN: 978-0-9839132-9-0.

LETTER FROM THE EDITORS:

THE SOCIAL NETWORK

"IF YOU USE an online social network," reads a recent lede in *Wired* magazine, "you give up a serious slice of your privacy thanks to the omnivorous way companies like Google and Facebook gather your personal data." The sentence reflects an assumption that is now widespread: that the problem of online privacy has to do with the vulnerability of our personal information to technology conglomerates. So conventional has this way of thinking become, at least among left-leaning intellectuals, that Dave Eggers has written a novel about it.

Whether or not warnings about what Evgeny Morozov calls the "growing commodification of our personal data" turn out to have been warranted, recent history suggests we will continue to ignore them. As a society we seem to have made a decision—and not one we can claim was uninformed—to continue using Google, Facebook and Amazon, regardless of the uses they might be making of our personal emails, web searches and shopping histories. As Thomas Meaney points out in this issue's symposium on privacy, recent revelations about the unprecedented (and sometimes illegal) information-gathering capabilities of internet companies, not to mention the U.S. government, have inspired a series of localized and academic protests, rather than (what might be expected, given the tenor of those protests) any kind of mass egress from the online portals where most of the spying is presumed to be taking place. Whatever the long-term risks of such activities, they have not struck most of us as severe enough to sacrifice, or even to seriously consider sacrificing, the conveniences of online commerce and communication.

That does not mean that we do not grapple every day with urgent privacy-related problems on the internet; we do. But the question we actually face in our daily lives is not how much personal or "private" information to share with Google, Facebook or Amazon—it is rather, and much more stressfully, how much of it to share with *our friends*.

THE CONVENTIONAL FRAMING of the online privacy problem assumes that our relationship with internet companies is based on a *contract*. "Since the rise of what was called Internet 2.0 about a decade ago," writes Reed

Hundt for a recent forum on privacy in the *Boston Review*, "nearly all Americans have shared their beliefs, values, social and commercial proclivities, and patterns of behavior with a handful of Web-based companies. In return, the companies—most prominently, Google, Facebook, Yahoo, and Amazon—have shared with everyone and profited fantastically from user-generated content provided both consciously (such as emails or Instagram photos) and unwittingly (such as location information tracked via cell phones)."

The contract model seems appropriate because it corresponds to the way we are accustomed to thinking of the individual's relationship with liberal society more generally. The most compelling accounts of how that contract is supposed to work were given by Hobbes, Locke and Rousseau in the seventeenth and eighteenth centuries. According to their social contract theories, all of which begin with a human being alone in a "state of nature," the individual sacrifices her natural privacy or freedom in return for security and a catalogue of material conveniences (property, nourishment, Netflix). The best society, on this model, is the one that offers us the most benefits and security while infringing the least on our independence. But even in the best society the contract has to be vigilantly policed; it is always possible for instance that the State, in the name of security, could violate the terms of the contract, as is often claimed to have happened in the case of the NSA wiretapping program.

Those who argue that Facebook and Google infringe unacceptably on our online privacy implicitly contend that the contracts we have entered into with social media companies, like the contract we enter into with our societies at large, can become either unfavorable or unfair. The contracts become *unfavorable* to the degree that any benefit we receive from using the networks is outweighed by what we have given up to become a part of them, and *unfair* to the degree that the companies themselves make it hard for us to understand what it is we have given up. This type of argument assumes that our relationship with online companies involves us in such subtle forms of exposure (we "unwittingly" divulge location information, says Hundt) that it is virtually impossible for us to take into account all the ways our privacy will eventually be violated.

Yet there is a problem with the extension of social contract theory to social media. The traditional social contract theorists always had a plausible explanation for why an individual would sacrifice her privacy or freedom—she was scared to death, for example, or hungry—in order to join society. But the same logic does not explain why contemporary individuals join online social networks. Looking for an equivalent, some have insisted that social networks confer essential economic benefits, or that social life is now impossible without them. Such claims are unconvincing. Many people conduct perfectly successful social and professional lives without joining social networks (you probably even know some of them); meanwhile, a flood of studies and books on the topic have confirmed what many of us already suspected from personal experience: that social networks do at least as much to erode our sense of well-being as to promote it.

So why, notwithstanding all the grave warnings, do informed people (more and more of them all the time) continue to join social networks and then to stay on them? Perhaps the growth of social networks demonstrates the importance of a desire the social contract theorists tended not to make much of—and which, more often than not, seems to supersede our desire for privacy or independence: the desire, that is, to be social.

W RITING A LITTLE later than the classic social contract theorists, Hegel offered a starkly different account of man's relationship with society. If the social contract theorists conjured an image of a self-sufficient individual seeking security and various practical advantages from society, Hegel imagined "natural" man as craven and slavish, largely indistinguishable from the other animals. For Hegel, we can only speak properly of "man" when we consider him already enmeshed in social relations, which enable him to address his craving for *recognition*.

Recognition is a key term in Hegel's political philosophy. Instead of imagining a bargain being struck between society and an individual bearing various "rights" (like the right to privacy), Hegel emphasizes that the concept of rights is empty until we consider the individual in a context where there exist people and institutions capable of recognizing those rights, as well as the full humanity of the person bearing them. This is the deepest reason why Hegel does not share Marx's or Rousseau's view that modern history is a story of decline, much less (as Stephen Dedalus puts it in *Ulysses*) a "nightmare." History for Hegel is intrinsically progressive, insofar as it is driven by a continuous negotiation between our self-understanding as individuals and the image we see reflected back to us by the people and institutions we look to for recognition. If the gap between my self-understanding and my society's understanding of me grows too wide (if I know I am an artist, but my society does not recognize me as one), this is a cause of dissatisfaction, and therefore a stimulus either to change society or to adjust my idea of myself.

This process of negotiation and adjustment can be seen at the heart of the most successful form of progressive politics in the previous half-century: identity politics. The ambition of identity politics has often been to bring society's view of a certain group into harmony with that group's view of itself. This includes lobbying to change laws—but also attitudes, conventions and popular opinion. It is important to note, however, something Hegel emphasized but which we often ignore today: that recognition is a two-way street. In attempting to bring society closer to their self-understanding, an individual or group might also be compelled, in light of their engagement with other individuals or groups, to revise that self-understanding. Society's view of me can be mistaken, but so too can my view of myself (if no one recognizes me as an artist, perhaps I am not in fact an artist).

That social networks require the exposure of personal information merely marks them as forums for social life—meaning places we go to engage in the "struggle" (as Hegel liked to put it) to achieve recognition. No matter where it is joined, that struggle *always* requires us to consider what we are willing to make public about ourselves, and to whom. From a Hegelian perspective, however, the first question about a social institution is not whether it compromises some pre-existing "right to privacy." What determines the institution's value is how well it mediates between our image of ourselves and the image that is held of us by our society—or, in the case of social networks, by our "followers" or "friends."

ON THE SURFACE, Facebook appears to provide ideal conditions for securing social recognition. It is convenient, easy to use, and everyone we know is always on it. Like any social platform, it discourages us from making certain choices, and incentivizes some types of exposure over others. Yet it grants us a wide freedom. Facebook asks us to pick which information to share; it gives us several options about how to share it; and it is perfectly satisfied if we decide to share nothing at all.

Indeed this freedom is the most difficult thing about Facebook: What to do with it? The weight of the responsibility can be hinted at by the fact that celebrities turn the task over to teams of professionals. But celebrities, thanks to Facebook, are no longer the only ones who are expected to become experts in public relations or what is sometimes called "image crafting." There are levels of this kind of thing, of course, but assuming you use Facebook for anything besides keeping up with your friends' birthdays and playing Candy Crush, there is nothing else you *can* do besides attempt to craft an appealing image of yourself. This is not due to personal vanity or commercialism; it simply indicates what Facebook is for.

Our most popular social network was invented, remember, by an awkward teenager with acute social anxiety and (by all accounts) an inferiority complex. Toward the beginning of David Fincher's *The Social Network* (2010), the Mark Zuckerberg character promises that he is about to "take the entire social experience of college and put it online." The movie has already established, however, that the social experience of college is painful for Zuckerberg—which is one reason he might ultimately be less interested in reproducing that experience than in escaping from it. What Zuckerberg actually creates is an alternative space where he can promote a carefully curated image of himself, one that accentuates his strengths and whitewashes his flaws. Nerdiness, physical weakness, even being an asshole in person are all subordinated, on Facebook, to one's talent for calculated self-presentation (a triumph of *ressentiment* if ever there was one!). The conventional wisdom that Facebook inspires gratuitous self-exposure does not simply overstate the danger; it inverts it. By allowing the individual to conceal and reveal at will, Facebook takes what used to be known as the public self and quietly recasts it in accordance with private fantasy.

Recent attempts to supplant Facebook, or at least parts of it, have nevertheless proceeded from the assumption that Facebook is *not private enough*. The much-discussed Ello will not compel members to share their real names at all, a feature that has been welcomed by those who find Facebook's sole limitation on anonymity to be unreasonably intrusive. An application called Whisper—in the news for feeding secrets to the U.S. military—advertises itself as allowing people to anonymously share "the behind-the-scenes stuff that we're not always comfortable posting on Facebook." Both claim to make people less wary of exposing unflattering personal information—either to their friends, or to corporations that might profit from it—than they would be on Facebook, but they achieve this objective by separating the information from its bearer. Like Facebook, only in reverse, Ello and Whisper promise to deliver their users the benefits of social life without exposing them to its risks.

Paradoxically, then, our existing social networks turn out to be anti-social: they all represent ways of avoiding—rather than participating in—the struggle for recognition. This struggle can certainly be embarrassing, or uncomfortable, just as Socrates thought genuine education would always be. For Hegel, such discomfort was sometimes necessary, on both a personal and a cultural level, if progress was to be made toward the end state of "absolute freedom," where individuals would finally grant one another reciprocal recognition and be able therefore to enjoy what Robert Pippin has called "the satisfactions of self-consciousness." Of course it would not be easy to reach such a resting place (even if Hegel believed it had been reached in late-nineteenth century Prussia—a debate for another time); it was nevertheless, Hegel thought, the only aspiration truly worthy of a social animal.

But if the motor of history is the discomfort caused by the gap between our own self-understandings and the way we find ourselves understood by others, then there is surely another, less sanguine way in which history might stop. What need is there to improve society, or ourselves, when we can simply reconfigure our personas at will on Facebook? Being recognized for doing cool things on weekends ("Steve has checked in at the Four Seasons Hotel Hong Kong!"; "Kira just finished the Turkey Trot!") might seem like a shallow form of gratification, but it is at least a reliable one—and, like more conventional intoxicants, we seem always to crave more of it. History would thus end, rather peacefully, with our becoming a nation of Zuckerbergs, bewitched behind our computer screens by the frictionless satisfactions of self-creation.

T HANKFULLY WE DO not (yet) live full-time on the internet, so there remain other avenues besides social networks for us to carry on our quest for recognition. By way of habituation, however—not to mention dissemination—social networks seem to be influencing how we engage in social life offline as well as on it. When we complain that contemporary politics have become an "echo chamber," we are objecting in part to political life becoming more and more like Facebook—a series of sheltered silos where our beliefs about ourselves and the world are flattered rather than challenged. Likewise the ongoing fragmentation of literary culture makes it less likely that we will read books or articles that threaten our self-understanding, or that our cultural habits will ever be subjected to criticism (if A. O. Scott is to be believed, it is now impossible to object even to adults reading "novels" written for their children). In academia, supposedly a bastion of vigorous debate, new arguments are greeted—by a dwindling and ever-more specialized audience—with a mixture of courtly congratulation and inward shrugs.

It is as if we have all gotten too accustomed to being out on Wittgenstein's "slippery ice, where there is no friction and so in a certain sense the conditions are ideal, but also, just because of that, we are unable to walk." Privacy, whatever its importance as a legal and political safeguard, has also become one of the ritualistic abstractions we invoke whenever someone suggests that we stop skating. But the point is to walk.

"Back to the rough ground!"

essays

Carp Matthew, *Preaching*, 2013

HELL

THE NEW STRATEGY FOR DEALING WITH DAMNATION

by Meghan O'Gieblyn

A COUPLE OF YEARS ago, a Chicago-based corporate-identity consultant named Chris Herron gave himself the ultimate challenge: rebrand hell. It was half gag, half self-promotion, but Herron took the project seriously, considering what it would take in the travel market for a place like hell to become a premier destination. The client was the Hell Office of Travel and Tourism (HOTT), which supposedly hired Herron in the wake of a steady decline in visitors caused by "a stale and unfocused brand strategy." After toying with some playfully sinful logos—the kind you might find on skater/goth products—Herron decided that what the locale needed to stay competitive in the afterlife industry was a complete brand overhaul. The new hell would feature no demons or devils, no tridents or lakes of fire. The brand name was rendered in lowercase, bubbly blue font, a wordmark designed to evoke "instant accessibility and comfort." The slogan—which had evolved from "Abandon Hope All Ye Who Enter Here" (1819) to "When You've Been Bad, We've Got It Good" (1963) to "Give in to Temptation" (2001)—would be "Simply Heavenly." The joke was posted as a "case study" on Herron's personal website and quickly went viral in the marketing blogosphere—a testament to the power of effective branding.

I grew up in an evangelical community that wasn't versed in these kinds of sales-pitch seductions. My family belonged to a dwindling Baptist congregation in southeast Michigan, where Sunday mornings involved listening to our pastor unabashedly preach something akin to the 1819 version of hell—a real diabolical place where sinners suffered for all eternity. In the late 1980s, when most kids my age were performing interpretive dances to "The Greatest Love of All" and receiving enough gold stars to fill a minor galaxy, my peers and I sat in Sunday school each week, memorizing scripture like 1 Peter 5:8: "Be self-controlled

13

and alert. Your enemy the devil prowls around like a roaring lion looking for someone to devour."*

I was too young and sheltered to recognize this worldview as anachronistic. Even now as an adult, it's difficult for me to hear biblical scholars like Elaine Pagels refer to Satan as "an antiquarian relic of a superstitious age," or to come across an aside, in a magazine or newspaper article, that claims the Western world stopped believing in a literal hell *during the Enlightenment*. My parents often attributed chronic sins like alcoholism or adultery to "spiritual warfare," (as in, "Let's remember to pray for Larry, who's struggling with spiritual warfare") and taught me and my siblings that evil was a real force that was in all of us. Our dinner conversations sounded like something out of a Hawthorne novel.

According to Christian doctrine, all human beings, believers included, are sinners by nature. This essentially means that no one can get through life without committing at least one moral transgression. In the eleventh century, Saint Anselm of Canterbury defined original sin as "privation of the righteousness that every man ought to possess." Although the "saved" are forgiven of their sins, they're never cured. Even Paul the Apostle wrote, "Christ Jesus came into the world to save sinners—*of whom I am the worst*." According to this view, hell isn't so much a penitentiary for degenerates as it is humanity's default destination. But there's a way out through accepting Christ's atonement, which, in the Protestant tradition, involves saying the sinner's prayer. For contemporary evangelicals, it's solely this act that separates the sheep from the goats. I've heard more than one believer argue that Mother Teresa is in hell for not saying this prayer, while Jeffrey Dahmer, who supposedly accepted Christ weeks before his execution, is in heaven.

I got saved when I was five years old. I have no memory of my conversion, but apparently my mom led me through the prayer, which involves confessing that you are a sinner and inviting Jesus into your heart. She might have told me about hell that night, or maybe I already knew it existed. Having a frank family talk about eternity was seen as a responsibility not unlike warning your kids about drugs or unprotected sex. It was uncomfortable, but preferable to the possible consequences of not doing so. Many Protestants believe that once a person is saved, it's impossible for her to lose her eternal security—even if she renounces her faith—so there's an urgency to catch kids before they start to ask

---

* I think evangelicals are under the impression that any scriptural passage with an animal reference is kid-friendly. In fact, this verse once inspired my Christian camp counselors to have our second-grade class sing a version of the doo-wop classic "The Lion Sleeps Tonight," as "The Devil Sleeps Tonight," which we performed for our parents, cheerily snapping our fingers and chanting "*awimbawe, awimbawe*," etc.

questions. Most of the kids I grew up with were saved before they'd lost their baby teeth.

For those who'd managed to slip between the cracks, the scare tactics started in earnest around middle school. The most memorable was *Without Reservation*, a thirty-minute video that I was lucky enough to see at least half a dozen times over the course of my teens. The film (which begins with the disclaimer: "The following is an abstract representation of actual events and realities") has both the production quality and the setup of a driver's ed video: five teens are driving home from a party, after much merrymaking, when their car gets broadsided by a semi. There's a brief montage of sirens and police radio voice-overs. Then it cuts to four of the kids, Bill, Ken, John and Mary, waking up in the car, which is mysteriously suspended in space. Below them is a line hundreds of people long, leading up to a man with white hair, stationed behind a giant IBM. When a person reaches the front of the line, this man (who's probably supposed to be God or St. Peter, but looks uncannily like Bob Barker) types the person's name into a DOS-like database, bringing up their photo, cause of death, and one of two messages: "Reservation Confirmed," or "Reservation Not Confirmed." He then instructs them to step to either the left or the right.

At this point, it's pretty clear that this isn't a film about the dangers of operating under the influence. The kids begin to realize that they're dead. One of them, Bill, a Christian, uneasily explains to the others that what they're seeing is a judgment line, at which point Mary loses it, shaking uncontrollably and sobbing "I want to go back! Why can't we all just go back!" The rest of the film consists of a long sequence showing their memorial service, back on earth, where some kind of school administrator speaks in secular platitudes about death being a place of safety and peace—a eulogy that is inter-spliced with shots of Ken, John and Mary learning that their reservation is "not confirmed," then being led down a red-lit hall and violently pushed into caged elevators. The last shot of them is in these cells—Mary curled in the fetal position, Ken and John pounding on the chain-link walls—as they descend into darkness. There's a little vignette at the end in which the fifth, surviving, passenger gets saved in the school cafeteria, but by that point I was always too shell-shocked to find it redemptive.

It's difficult to overstate the effect this film had on my adolescent psyche. Lying in bed at night, I replayed the elevator scene over and over in my head, imagining what fate lay in store for those kids and torturing myself with the possibility that I might be one of the unconfirmed. What if I had missed a crucial part of the prayer? Or what if God's computer got some kind of celestial virus and my name was erased? When you get saved young, when you have no life transformation—no rugged past to turn from—the prayer itself carries real power, like a hex.*

This anxiety was exacerbated by the fact that, around junior high, youth leaders began urging us to "re-invite" Christ into our lives. They insinuated that those of us who had been saved early might not have *actually* been saved—particularly if we were just repeating obediently after our parents. Some said the childhood prayers had been provisional, a safety net until we reached the age of accountability (traditionally believed to be twelve). Apparently, the words weren't enough—you had to mean them, and, at least to some extent, you had to live them. Good works couldn't get you into heaven, but if your life showed no sign of the Holy Spirit working in you, then this was a pretty good hint that you might not have been completely genuine when you asked Jesus into your life.

One of the most obvious ways of living your faith was through evangelism. I recently re-watched *Without Reservation* and realized that, as a kid, I'd totally missed the intended message. The film was not a scare tactic meant to trick teens into becoming Christians; it was very clearly designed for the already-saved, a dramatized pep talk urging us to get the word out about hell to our non-Christian friends. The most dramatic sequence of the film (apart from the elevators) is when John, before being carried off to hell, asks Bill, the believer, why he never said anything about eternal damnation. "We rode home from practice together every day," he pleads. "We talked about a lot of stuff, but we never talked about this." Bill can only offer feeble excuses like "I thought you weren't interested!" and "I thought there was more time!"

That this message never got across to me might have had something to do with the fact that, as a homeschooled junior-high student, I actually didn't know any unbelievers. In my mind, the "lost" consisted of a motley minority of animal-worshipping tribesmen, Michael Jackson, Madonna, and our Catholic neighbors. It wasn't until I started going to public high school that I began to feel a gnawing guilt, spurred by the occasional realization that my evolution-touting biology teacher, or the girl who sat next to me in study hall reading *The Satanic Bible*, was going to spend eternity suffering. Despite this, I never got up the courage to share my faith. Part of it was a lack of personal conviction. But I

---

* At one point during my early teens, before I understood the concept of eternal security, it occurred to me that if I could ask Jesus into my heart, I could just as easily ask him to leave. Once this fear lodged itself in my brain, it became impossible not to think the prayer "Jesus, go out of my heart," the way it's impossible not to visualize a purple hippopotamus once someone tells you not to. For weeks, I found myself mentally replaying this heresy, then immediately correcting it with the proper salvation prayer, all the while terrified that something would happen to me (a car accident, a brain aneurysm) in the seconds in between, while I was technically unsaved.

was also becoming aware that the gospel message—which depends on convincing a person he's a sinner in need of God's grace—sounded seriously offensive and self-righteous. Our pastor always said that we needed to speak about hell in a spirit of love, but he clearly didn't know what it was like to be a teenager in the 1990s. I went to a high school that didn't publish the honor roll for fear of hurting those who weren't on it. The most popular yearbook quote among my graduating class was Tupac's "Only God can judge me." And most of those kids didn't even believe in God.

In retrospect, *Without Reservation* looks to me like a last-ditch effort, one of the church's final attempts to convince the emerging generation of the need to speak candidly about eternity. Over the course of my teenage years, Christians began to slip into awkward reticence about the doctrine of damnation. Believers still talked about the afterlife, but the language was increasingly euphemistic and vague. People who rejected Jesus were "eternally separated from God." We were saved not from an infinity of torment, but from "the bondage of sin." Back then, nobody in ministry had the hubris—nor, probably, the sophistication—to rebrand hell à la Chris Herron. Rather, hell was relegated to the margins of the gospel message, the fine print on the eternal-life warranty.

I N THE KING James Bible, the English word "hell" serves as the translation of four different Greek and Hebrew terms. The Old Testament refers exclusively to *Sheol*, the traditional Hebrew underworld, a place of stillness in which both the righteous and the unrighteous wander in shadows. There's no fiery torment, no wailing or gnashing of teeth. The devil had not yet been invented (though Satan, a trickster angel with whom he would later be conflated, pops up now and then). Sinners seem remarkably off the hook—so much so that Job laments that the wicked "spend their days in prosperity and in peace they go down to Sheol." For many of these writers, the word simply denotes its literal translation, "grave," or unconscious death. The psalmist prays, "For in death there is no remembrance of thee: in Sheol who shall give thee thanks?"

In the New Testament, several writers refer to this place under its Greek name, *Hades*. There's also a number of passages about *Gehenna*, literally "the Valley of Hinnom," which was a real area outside Jerusalem that served as the city dump. Fires burned there constantly, to incinerate the garbage; it was also a place where the bodies of criminals were burned. The Jewish rabbinical tradition envisioned Gehenna as a purgatorial place of atonement for the ungodly. This is the word Jesus uses when he gives the hyperbolic command that one

Carp Matthew, *Conjoined Mutants Fighting over a Box of
Chicken Skin in the Abandoned Cathedral*, 2010

should cut off the hand that is causing one to sin: "It is better for thee to enter into life maimed, than having two hands to go into Gehenna, into the fire that never shall be quenched." Another Greek term, *Tartarus*, appears only once, when the author of 1 Peter writes about the angel rebellion that took place before the creation of the world. Drawing from the Greek myth of the Olympians overthrowing the Titans, he relays how Lucifer and his allies were cast out of heaven into Tartarus. In the *Aeneid*, Virgil describes Tartarus as a place of torment guarded by the Hydra and surrounded by a river of fire to prevent the escape of condemned souls. Except in the 1 Peter version, there are no human souls there, just bad angels.

The most dramatic descriptions of hell come from the strain of apocalyptic literature that runs through the New Testament, as well as the Old Testament prophets. Apocalypticism was a worldview that arose during the sixth century BCE, when Israel was under Syrian domination. It involved the belief that the present era, which was ruled by evil, would soon give way to a new age here on earth in which God would restore justice and all evildoers would be punished. The authors of Daniel and Ezekiel were apocalyptists—so was John of Patmos, the author of Revelation. It's these authors who provide us with passages such as, "They will be tormented with burning sulfur in the presence of the holy angels and of the Lamb. And the smoke of their torment will rise for ever and ever." This was a belief system born out of persecution. The Book of Daniel was written in response to the oppressive monarch Antiochus Epiphanes; the Book of Revelation came about during the rule of Domitian, who had Christians burned, crucified and fed to wild animals. As Nietzsche noted in *The Genealogy of Morals*, these passages are essentially revenge fantasies, written by people who'd suffered horrible injustices and had no hope of retribution in this life. In fact, many of the fantastical beasts that populate these books were meant to represent contemporary rulers like Nero or Antiochus.

I didn't learn any of this at church. As a kid, it never occurred to me that Solomon and Daniel had drastically different views about the afterlife. Christian theology, as it has developed over the centuries, has functioned like a narrative gloss, smoothing the irregular collection of biblical literature into a cohesive story written by a single, divine author. Secular scholars refer to this as "the myth," the story that depicts all of human history as an epic of redemption. Paul came up with the idea of original sin, transforming the Crucifixion into a voluntary sacrifice that brought salvation to the world. Drawing from his background as a Pharisee, he connected Hebrew scripture to the life of Christ. Just as sin entered the world through one man, Adam, so can the world be redeemed by the death of one man. As time went on, Satan, Lucifer and Beelzebub were consolidated into a single entity, the personification of all evil. Likewise Sheol, Gehenna,

Hades and Tartarus came to be understood as physical representations of the darkest place in the universe. By the time the King James Bible was published in the sixteenth century, each of these words was translated as simply "hell."

The various depictions of hell over the centuries tend to mirror the earthly landscape of their age. Torture entered the conception of hell in the second century, when Christians were subjected to sadistic public spectacles. Roman interrogation methods included red-hot metal rods, whips and the rack—a contraption that distended limbs from their joints. The non-canonical *Apocalypse of Peter*, a product of this era, features a fierce and sadistic hell in which people are blinded by fire and mangled by wild beasts. Dante's *Divine Comedy* has traces of the feudal landscape of fourteenth-century Europe. Lower hell is depicted as a walled city with towers, ramparts, bridges and moats; fallen angels guard the citadel like knights. The Jesuits, who rose to prominence during a time of mass immigration and urban squalor, envisioned an inferno of thousands of diseased bodies "pressed together like grapes in a wine-press." It was a claustrophobic hell without latrines, and part of the torture was the human stench.

Today, biblical literalists believe hell exists outside of time and space, in some kind of spiritual fifth dimension. Contemporary evangelical churches don't display paintings or stained glass renderings of hell. It's no longer a popular subject of art. If hell is represented at all, it's in pop culture, where it appears as either satirically gaudy—like animated Hieronymus Bosch—or else eerily banal. In *The Far Side*, Satan and his minions are depicted as bored corporate drones who deal with the scourge of the post-industrial earth. ("There's an insurance salesman here," Satan's secretary says. "Should I admit him or tell him to go to Heaven?") One of the most popular diabolical archetypes in recent years has been the effete Satan. He shows up in episodes of *The Simpsons* and appears in Tenacious D videos, whining about the fine print of the Demon Code. He makes cameos in *South Park*, where he's usually involved in petty domestic squabbles with his boyfriend, Saddam Hussein. Satan has become an unwelcome nuisance, an impotent archetype occasionally dragged out for a good laugh. In an episode of *Saturday Night Live* from 1998, Garth Brooks plays a struggling musician who tries to sell his soul to the devil for a hit song, only to find that Satan (Will Ferrell) is an even more pathetic songwriter than he. When Satan finally gives up and asks if he can leave, Garth shows him out and tells him to lock the door behind him.

Although the sermons of my childhood were often set against the backdrop of hell, I wasn't introduced to the theological doctrine of damnation until I enrolled at Moody Bible Institute at the age of eighteen. Known within evangelical circles as the "West Point of Christian service," Moody is one of the most conservative Christian colleges in the country. When I was there, students weren't allowed to dance, watch movies or be alone in a room with a member of the opposite sex. The campus was downtown, occupying a purgatorial no man's land between the luxurious Gold Coast and the Cabrini-Green housing projects, but most of the students rarely left campus. The buildings were connected by subterranean tunnels, so it was possible to spend months, particularly in the winter, going from class to the dining hall to the dorms, without ever stepping outside. We spent our free time quizzing one another on Greek homework, debating predestination over soft-serve ice cream at the Student Center, and occasionally indulging in some doctrinal humor (Q: What do you call an Arminian whale? A: Free Willy).

Ideologically, Moody is a peculiar place. Despite the atmosphere of serious scholarship, the institute is theologically conservative, meaning that we studied scripture not as a historic artifact, but as the Word of God. Most of the professors thought the world was created in six days. Nearly all of them believed in a literal hell. One of the most invidious tasks of the conservative theologian is to explain how a loving God can allow people to suffer for all of eternity. God is omnipotent and Paul claims it is his divine will that all people should be saved—yet hell exists. Before taking freshman Systematic Theology, I'd never given this problem much thought, but once I considered it, it seemed pretty significant. In layman's terms, the argument our professors gave us went something like this: God is holy by nature and cannot allow sin into his presence (i.e. into heaven). He loves all humans—in fact, he loves them so much that he gave them free will, so that they could choose to refuse salvation. In this way, people essentially condemned themselves to hell. God wasn't standing over the lake of fire, laughing uproariously while casting souls into the flames. Hell was simply the dark side of the universe, the yin to God's yang, something that must exist for there to be universal justice.*

There were still a number of problems with this formulation, but for the most part I was willing to suspend my disbelief and trust that God's ways were higher than my own. What bothered me was the numbers. Freshman year, every student was required to take a seminar called Christian Missions. It was basically a history of international evangelism, taught by Dr. Elizabeth Lightbody, a six-foot-three retired missionary to the Philippines who sported a topiary of

---

* There's a widespread misconception that biblical literalism is facile and mindless, but the doctrine I was introduced to at Moody was every bit as complicated and arcane as Marxist theory or post-structuralism. There were students at the institute who got in fierce debates about infralapsarianism vs. supralapsarianism (don't ask) and considered devoting their lives to pneumatology (the study of the Holy Spirit). In many ways, Christian literalism is even *more* complicated than liberal brands of theology because it involves the sticky task of reconciling the overlay myth—the story of redemption—with a wildly inconsistent body of scripture.

gray-blonde curls, wore brightly colored wool suits and smiled so incessantly it seemed almost maniacal. During the first week of class, we watched a video that claimed there were currently 2.8 billion people among "the unreached"—that is, people who had never heard the gospel. Dr. Lightbody, like the rest of the faculty, adhered to exclusivism, the belief that only those with faith in Jesus Christ can be saved (as opposed to pluralism, the belief that people of all religions will be saved, regardless of the name they use for God). Jesus said that "no man comes to the Father, but by me," and we had to take this word for word as the truth, meaning it included those who had no idea who Jesus was.* Technically, I'd known this since I was a kid (after all, if the unreached could get to heaven some other way, what would be the point of sending missionaries?), but I'd never paused to consider the implications. If you took into consideration all the people who'd ever lived—including those centuries upon centuries when entire continents were cut off from the spread of Christianity—then the vast majority of humanity was going to spend eternity in hell.

I tried to feel out other students to see if anyone else was having similar thoughts, but it was a dangerous subject. Our communal language was so rigid and coded that there was very little vocabulary with which to express doubt. I had to frame my questions as technical doctrinal queries, or else pretend I was seeking evangelism advice (e.g. "Say an unbeliever were to ask you to defend the existence of hell..."). One evening, in the cafeteria, I suggested that it seemed kind of unfair that people were going to suffer for eternity simply because we believers hadn't managed to bring them the good news. On this point, I got nothing more than a thoughtful nod or a somber "hmm." A few students gave me knowing smiles and little shoulder squeezes, as though I was in the midst of some revelatory spiritual experience that would lead me to the mission field.

On Friday nights, I went down to Michigan Avenue with a dozen other students to do street evangelism. Our team leader was Zeb, a lanky, pimpled Missions major who probably would have been into LARPing or vampirism if he weren't a Christian. Instead, he memorized Luther and Zwingli and made vivid chalk drawings illustrating the plan of salvation, all of which made him kind of popular on campus. We'd set up an easel in front of Banana Republic, and Zeb would draw the abyss that lies between mankind and God, which can only be bridged by the cross, telling the story of redemption as he drew. The rest of us handed out tracts to tourists and businesspeople. We usually drew a

---

* One day, a student asked about children who died without being saved. Dr. Lightbody gave an answer so tortured and evasive that I had no clue what she was implying until she closed with the caveat "Now, don't ever say that to a mother who's lost a baby." I later found out that Augustine also believed unbaptized infants were sent to hell.

small crowd—mostly men who were waiting for their wives to finish shopping and seemed to view us as a zany sideshow. It wasn't one of those vicious "turn or burn" productions, but Zeb's chalk narrative referred to sin and repentance, and the tracts, which had the reasonable title "How to Become a Christian," mentioned hell only once or twice. These terms were the water we swam in, but out on the street, against the softly lit backdrop of window displays, they sounded ancient and fierce.

I knew how ridiculous we looked. These people already knew who Jesus was. They'd grown up watching Jerry Falwell spaz out on TV, or sneering at Ned Flanders on *The Simpsons*. They didn't know all the theological reasons why God was good, and would probably never give us the time of day to explain them. We were speaking a foreign language. In a just world, they wouldn't be held accountable for their refusal of the gospel any more than an unreached person who followed his culture's belief in ancestral worship. When Zeb gave the call to come forward and find forgiveness in Jesus Christ, our audience awkwardly glanced at their watches, put their headphones back on, or yawned.

W HILE I WAS attending Moody, the most controversial church in the Chicago area was Willow Creek Community Church, out in the northwest suburbs. I'd heard students raving about it—and others railing against it—ever since orientation week. It was popular amongst the Pastoral, Youth Ministry and Sports Ministry majors. The critics were mostly in the theology department. Willow Creek's pastor, Bill Hybels, was a well-known author and something of a celebrity in the evangelical world, but the big draw was apparently the size of the church. There was a $73 million "Worship Center," a food court and a parking lot worthy of an international airport. Every Sunday morning, a school bus would pull up to the Moody campus and dozens of students would climb on board to be bused out to South Barrington for the 9 a.m. service. I had been attending a fledgling Baptist church in Uptown that year, and when I got back to the school cafeteria on Sunday afternoons I was routinely confronted with students fresh off the Willow Creek bus, all of whom were visibly charged, as though they'd just gotten back from a rock concert. One blustery Sunday morning in February, as I was walking to the "L" station to catch the train to Uptown, faced with the prospect of another 65-minute sermon about gratitude or long-suffering, I found myself suddenly veering across the campus to get on the Willow Creek bus.

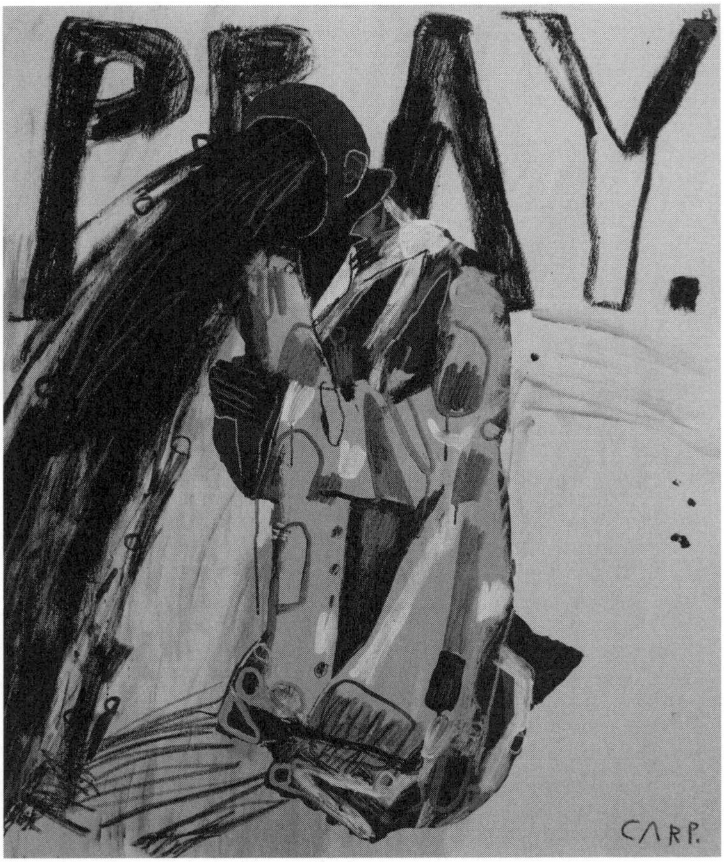
PRAY.
CARP.

Carp Matthew, *Pray*, 2012

I'd always associated megachurches with televangelists, those bottle-tanned preachers with Southern accents who addressed the cameras from palatial churches with fountains out front. Willow Creek was different. The Worship Center seated 7,000 people, but it was sleek and spare, more convention hall than cathedral. Hybels preached in a simple oxford shirt, and his charisma was muted, reminiscent of the gentle authority assumed by dentists and family physicians. The sermon was based in scripture. At first, it just seemed like the traditional gospel set to a brighter tempo. According to Hybels, God's love was not an unearned gift granted to sinners, but proof that we mattered on a cosmic scale. Our primary fault was not our sinful nature, but our tendency to think too little of ourselves. We needed to expand our vision, to stop doubting that we could do amazing things for God. It took me several more visits, over the following few months, before I was able to put my finger on what was off. One Sunday, as I was riding back on the bus, staring out at the mirror-plated corporate headquarters along the freeway, I realized that I couldn't recall anyone at Willow Creek ever mentioning sin, repentance or confession. I never once heard a reference to hell.

I wasn't aware of it at the time, but Willow Creek was on the front lines of a movement some described as a "second Reformation," with the potential to remake the Christian faith. Hybels was one of a handful of pastors—including, most notably, Rick Warren of Saddleback Church in California (author of *The Purpose Driven Life*)—who pioneered what would become known as the "seeker-friendly church," a congregation targeting the vast population of Americans who had little to no experience with Christianity ("unchurched Harry and Mary," in ministry lingo). The goal was to figure out why this demographic was turned off by the gospel, and then to create a worship service that responded to their perceived needs.

Essentially, this is consumer-based management.* During Willow Creek's inception, Hybels—who studied business before entering the ministry—performed preliminary market research, surveying the unreligious in his community to find out why people weren't going to church. Unsurprisingly, the most common responses were "church is boring," "I don't like being preached down to" and "it makes me feel guilty." Harry and Mary were made uncomfortable by overt religious symbolism and archaic language. They didn't like being bombarded by welcome committees. The solution was a more positive message: upbeat tunes, an emphasis on love and acceptance. There would be respect for anonym-

---

* Hybels keeps a poster in his office that reads: "What is our business? Who is our customer? What does the customer consider value?" Rick Warren's Saddleback motto is "Let the target audience determine the approach."

ity—visitors wouldn't be required to wear name tags or stand up and introduce themselves. Everything was designed for the visitor's comfort and leisure.

It goes without saying that pastors who are trying to "sell" God won't mention hell any more than a Gap ad will call attention to child labor. Under the new business model, hell became the meatpacking plant, the sweatshop, the behind-the-scenes horror the consumer doesn't want to know about. Once I became aware of what was missing, it was almost a game to watch the ministers try to maneuver around the elephant in the room. One strategy was to place the focus exclusively on heaven, letting people mentally fill in the blank about the alternative. Another was to use contemporary, watered-down translations of the Bible, like *The Message* (reviled around Moody's theology department, where it was better known as "The Mess").

Some Moody students accused Hybels of being a Universalist—a charge lodged against Rick Warren as well, based on his refusal to mention the h-word. But away from the pulpit, these ministers were surprisingly traditional. In his book *Honest to God?* Hybels writes, "I hate thinking about it, teaching about it, and writing about it. But the plain truth is that hell *is* real and real people go there for eternity." Warren admitted essentially the same thing when pressed in an interview: "I believe in a literal hell. Jesus believed in a literal hell. And once you're in, you can't get out." This raises the obvious question: How ethical is it to stand up each week before an audience who you believe are going to suffer for all of eternity, and not talk about hell because you "hate thinking about it," or are afraid people will be offended?

At the same time, I realized that Hybels and Warren were responding to the problem we'd noticed down on Michigan Avenue. Most of my friends at Moody disagreed with their approach, but our only other option was to be the ranting voice in the wilderness. It was a hopeless effort, and we all knew it. People looked at our street evangelism team like we were Jesus freaks. (In fact, a number of passersby felt compelled to say as much.) Every Friday night, we'd ride back to campus on the subway in silence, each of us staring slack-faced at the crowd of people hooked up to MP3 players and engrossed in fashion magazines. Many of my friends were planning to leave the States after graduation to become missionaries to the developing world. Apparently it was easier to convince people of the existence of hell and the need for salvation in places like Uganda and Cambodia, where the human capacity for evil was more than an abstraction. Zeb was planning to go to Albania after graduation to plant churches, though he said he worried this was taking the easy way out, like Jonah jumping the boat to Tarsus to avoid bringing the news to the more affluent Nineveh. He said the U.S. had become so rich and powerful we'd forgotten our need for divine grace.

I STARTED MY SOPHOMORE year at Moody in September 2001. On the morning of the 11th, I'd overslept and woke up to my roommate—a soprano in the women's choir—shrieking that we'd been "bombed." There was one television in my dorm, on the second floor, and I made it down there to find the entire female student body crowded around it, watching the footage in silence. An hour later, we were filing into the eeriest chapel service of all time. The overhead lights were off and the television footage was projected onto a large screen at the front of the auditorium. The school president announced that instead of the regular session, we were going to hold a prayer hour, so we split off into circles, holding hands and whispering in the dark, beneath the muted apocalyptic footage. Nobody knew what to say. We were Bible school students—the closest thing to professional pray-ers out there—and yet people stumbled over common phrases and veered into awkward anachronisms like "keep us from evil" and "bestow thy grace." When it was my turn, I squeezed the hand of the girl next to me, signaling for her to go ahead. After the service, they turned the sound back on, but it seemed like the newscasters were just as dumbstruck as we were.

Once the initial shock wore off, you could sense people groping around the cultural junk drawer for appropriate terminology. Newscasters and witnesses referred to Ground Zero as an "inferno" and "hell on earth." In his address to the nation, George W. Bush said, "Today, our nation saw evil." It was a rhetorical choice designed "deliberately to seek an antique religious aura," as a writer for the *New York Times* noted. Biblical prophecy was revived by conspiracy theorists who tried to prove that the disaster was predicted in the Book of Daniel, or who claimed that the architect of the Twin Towers resided at 666 5th Avenue. A handful of people said they saw the face of Satan in the smoke billowing out of the World Trade Center. Very quickly, a makeshift theology of good and evil was patched together. The terrorists were "evildoers" who, as Colin Powell put it, were "conducting war against civilized people."

Evangelicals responded with similar vitriol. Billy Graham called the acts "twisted diabolical schemes," and the Church of the Open Door's David Johnson preached from the Book of Revelation, insinuating that the terrorists were a "demonic force in the earth." Around Moody, our professors and administrators kept talking about how the pilots must have been surprised when they woke up expecting to be welcomed by Allah and instead found themselves face-to-face with Jesus and the prospect of eternal suffering. This was said with a belabored sigh that often concealed, I suspected, a note of vindictive satisfaction.

That Sunday, Willow Creek was one of many American churches filled to the brim with newcomers. The Moody bus arrived a little late for the morning

Carp Matthew, *Grey Bastard*, 2007

service, and we ended up sitting in the uppermost balcony, looking down at the crowd of people seeking spiritual comfort. I was eager to see how Bill Hybels would handle the event—whether he would demonize the enemy or invoke safe platitudes about the brevity of life. As it turned out, he did something completely different. One of the biggest lessons of the past week, he began by saying, was that "evil is alive and well." It was the first time I'd heard the word from his pulpit.

Hybels then did something even more unexpected. He proposed that the evil we'd experienced was not limited to the men who flew the planes. He alluded to the terrorists' accomplices and the people in other countries who were shown celebrating the tragedy. Those actions were evil as well, he said. He talked about the gas station owners who'd tripled their prices to capitalize on the hysteria and the people who attacked Arab Americans out of rage. At this point, the audience hummed in collective disapproval.

The pastor paused for a moment, and then said, "Let's bring it close to home—what about the evil in me? Because boy, I felt it this week." Hybels then described his own anger when he was watching the news footage, his immediate craving for revenge. "What is it in us that makes some of us want others to pay a hundred times over for the wrong done to us?" he asked. "Well, that would be evil, and I felt it in me. Did you feel it in you?" With regard to the military response, he argued that Jesus's teaching to not repay evil with evil was just as relevant at a national level. Think about the retaliation that happened all over the world, he said: How was that working out for Sudan? How was it working out for Northern Ireland? The vindictive rage we felt watching the attacks from our kitchen televisions was the same emotion that was creating hell all over the world.

I hadn't felt that rage myself—not because of virtue or self-discipline, but because I was too immature to grasp the full scope of what had happened. It all seemed removed, cinematic. But I did know the feeling he was talking about. It was the same thing I felt when our evangelism team got called Bible-thumpers and Jesus freaks.

I don't know what prompted Hybels to diverge from the market-tested optimism that day, but it was a powerful sermon—people at Moody were talking about it all week. In fact, in a study on the evangelical response to 9/11, this sermon was cited as the only one that questioned the compatibility of military action with Jesus's command to love one's neighbor. The pacifism of the political Left seemed inert and self-flagellating by comparison. Their hesitance to condemn the terrorists, the insistence on the passive voice when describing what had happened, often made it seem as though the attacks had been an act of God, divine punishment for Western imperialism. That Sunday was the only time that someone had asked me to examine myself and my response to the attacks without dismissing their severity, or the reality of the human intention behind them. The next Sunday, Hybels preached a message entitled "Religion Gone Awry," about how the backlash against American Muslims ran counter to Christian principles. The following week, he invited Imam Faisal Hammouda to speak at the Sunday service, giving the congregation the opportunity to exercise "discernment" in understanding Islam.

One of the most perplexing things about 9/11, for me, was how swiftly the event congealed in and then dissipated from the national consciousness. Half a century ago, when Roosevelt addressed the country after Pearl Harbor, he underscored the severity of the offense by declaring that the nation would not forget it: "Always will we remember the character of the onslaught against us ... There is no blinking at the fact that our people, our territory and our interests are in grave danger." Since then, it seems we've come to see prolonged meditation on this kind of horror as a sign of weakness and a threat to the market. Less than two months after the attacks, Bush noted with pride, "People are going about their daily lives, working and shopping and playing, worshipping at churches and synagogues and mosques, going to movies and to baseball games."

Willow Creek soon got back to business as usual as well, mostly due to the huge backlash against Hybels's decision to "share his pulpit" (as his critics phrased it) with an imam. Apparently the honeymoon was over. People began to find tolerance tedious. Although Hybels didn't apologize for his decision to bring in the imam, he seemed, like any good CEO, to take note of the negative response. In the first sermon of 2002, he encouraged us to put the past year's events behind us and adopt, instead, "an optimistic hope-filled attitude for the year." It was the first message of a sermon series that included titles such as "Wellness," "Family" and "Surviving a Financial Storm." In the end, his radical sermons about collective evil turned out to be aberrational—like many noble acts inspired by the tragedy and then quickly forgotten.

AT THE TIME, I didn't appreciate just how radical Hybels's 9/11 sermon was. In speaking about his own capacity for revenge and hatred, he had opened up a possibility, a way of talking about evil that felt relevant and transformative. It wasn't fire and brimstone; it wasn't condemning the sinner as some degenerate Other. Rather, he was challenging his congregation to exercise empathy in a way that Jesus might have, suggesting that he among us without sin should cast the first stone.

Back at Moody, though, I was still staying up late at night, thinking about all those people who would suffer for eternity for never hearing the gospel. By the end of the semester, the problem of hell had begun to seriously unsettle my faith—so much so that I had lost the ability to perform the basic rites. When I stood in chapel with my classmates, I was unable to sing along to the hymns in praise of God's goodness; and when we bowed our heads to pray, I pantomimed that act of supplication. I left Moody the summer after my sophomore year and took a volunteer position with some missionaries in Ecuador, which was just an elaborate escape plan—a way to get away from Moody and my parents. Three months into the commitment, I moved to a town in the south of the country where I didn't know anyone and got a job teaching ESL. I ditched my study Bible at a hostel book exchange and stopped going to church entirely.

But people who've gotten that far into the faith never totally shake it. To be a former believer is to perpetually return to the scene of the crime. It's been ten years since I left Moody, and I still find myself stalling on the Christian radio station to hear a call-in debate, or lurking around the religion section of chain bookstores, perusing the titles on the Christianity shelves like a porn addict sneaking a glance at a Victoria's Secret catalog.

In the spring of 2011, I was browsing through a crowded airport news-stand when I glimpsed an issue of *Time* with the headline "What If There's No Hell?" The subhead elaborated, "A popular pastor's best-selling book has stirred fierce debate about sin, salvation, and judgment." The book in question was the modestly titled *Love Wins: Heaven, Hell, and the Fate of Every Person Who's Ever Lived*, and the pastor, it turned out, was Rob Bell. Back when I was at Moody, Bell was known primarily as the pastor of Mars Hill Bible Church in Grandville, Michigan—one of the more groundbreaking "seeker churches" in the Midwest. If Hybels was the entrepreneur of the seeker movement, Bell was its rock star. He wears hipster glasses and black skinny jeans and looks strikingly like Bono, if you can imagine the laconic machismo replaced with a kind of nerdy alacrity. Most of Bell's congregants were Gen Xers who had difficulty with the Bible's passages about absolute truth, certainty and judgment. His first book, *Velvet Elvis: Repainting the Christian Faith* (2005), was purportedly aimed at people who are "fascinated with Jesus but can't do the standard Christian package."

I found a copy of Bell's new book at that same airport and blew through it during my three-hour flight to Michigan. It was a light read. Bell lineates his prose like a free-verse poem, and roughly half the sentences are interrogative, a rhetorical style that seems designed to dampen the incendiary nature of his actual argument. He does not, as the *Time* headline suggests, make a case against the existence of hell. Rather, he argues that hell is a refining process by which all of the sins of the world, but not the sinners, are burned away. Those who

Carp Matthew, *Meditation*, 2013

are in hell are given endless chances throughout eternity to accept God's free gift of salvation and, because this gift is so irresistibly good, hell will eventually be emptied and collapse. Essentially, this is universal reconciliation—the idea that all people will be saved regardless of what they believe or how they conduct themselves on earth.

Love Wins created an uproar in the evangelical community. Zondervan (basically the Random House of Christian publishing), which had published Bell's previous books, dropped him upon reading the proposal, stating that the project didn't fit with their mission. After it was published, Albert Mohler, Jr., a prominent reformed pastor, called the book "theologically disastrous" and conservative John Piper tweeted "Farewell Rob Bell," as if to excommunicate him from the fold. Closer to home, Bell watched as thousands of his congregants left Mars Hill in protest. At the same time, a lot of evangelicals who seemed to have been harboring a private faith in universal reconciliation came out of the woodwork and defended the book. And in the secular media, the theology of *Love Wins* was lauded as the radical conception of a visionary. Bell was the subject of a long profile in the *New Yorker*, and *Time* named him one of the most influential people in the world. "Wielding music, videos and a Starbucks sensibility," the magazine wrote, "Bell is at the forefront of a rethinking of Christianity in America."

"Rethinking" is not as accurate as "rebranding." Throughout *Love Wins*, it's obvious that Bell is less interested in theological inquiry than he is in PR. At one point in the book, in order to demonstrate the marketing problems many congregations unwittingly create, he gives a sampling of "statements of faith" from various church websites, all of which depict a traditional Christian understanding of hell (e.g. "The unsaved will be separated forever from God in hell"). Instead of responding to these statements on a theological basis, he remarks, sarcastically, "Welcome to our church." Later on, he reiterates his warning that even the most sophisticated seeker churches won't succeed in attracting unbelievers unless they revamp their theology: "If your God is loving one second and cruel the next, if your God will punish people for all eternity for sins committed in a few short years, no amount of clever marketing or compelling language or good music or great coffee will be able to disguise that one, true, glaring, untenable, unacceptable, awful reality."

Despite Bell's weak hermeneutics and the transparency of his motivation, there was one moment while reading *Love Wins* where it seemed as though he might initiate a much-needed conversation about the meaning of hell. Toward the end of the book, he begins to mobilize a more radical argument—that heaven and hell are not realms of the afterlife but metaphors for life here on earth. "Heaven and hell [are] here, now, around us, upon us, within us," he writes. He recalls traveling to Rwanda in the early 2000s and seeing boys whose limbs had been cut off during the genocide. "Do I believe in a literal hell?" he asks. "Of course. Those aren't metaphorical missing arms and legs." Here, I brightened at the idea that perhaps Bell was out to make a statement as bold and daring as Hybels's 9/11 sermon, using hell as a way to talk about the human capacity for evil.

But no such moment came. As I read on, it became clear that Bell wasn't actually looking for a way to talk about the darker side of human nature. Soon after he posits the possibility of a metaphorical hell, he glosses over its significance by suggesting that the "hells" of this earth are slowly being winnowed away as humans work to remedy social problems like injustice and inequality. He suggests that Jesus's allusions to the Kingdom of God were referring not to an eternal paradise, but rather to an earthly golden age (a claim with which few—if any—evangelicals would agree, even if it is commonly accepted among secular scholars). In his discussion of Revelation, Bell skims over most of the apocalyptic horrors to note that the book ends with a description of "a new city, a new creation, a new world that God makes, right here in the midst of this one. It is a buoyant, hopeful vision of a future in which the nations are healed and there is peace on earth and there are no more tears." Traditionally, evangelicals have read the "new city" as representing heaven, but Bell's insistence that this new creation is "right in the midst of this one" suggests a kind of Hegelian linear-progressive history, a vision of the future in which humanity improves itself until we've engineered a terrestrial utopia. It's an echo of the contemporary narrative of technological solutionism—the gospel of human perfectability that is routinely hyped in TED talks and preached from the Lucite podiums of tech conferences across the country.

Love Wins succeeded in breaking the silence about hell, and its popularity suggests that a number of evangelicals may be ready to move beyond a literalist notion of damnation, reimagining hell just as God-fearing people across the centuries have done to reckon with the evils of their own age. At the same time, the book demonstrates the potential pitfalls of the church's desire to distance itself too quickly from fire and brimstone. Bell claims to address the exact theological problem that motivated me to leave the faith, but rather than offer a new understanding of the doctrine, he offers up a Disneyesque vision of humanity, one that is wholly incompatible with the language biblical authors use to speak about good and evil. Along with hell, the new evangelical leaders threaten to jettison the very notion of human depravity—a fundamental Christian truth upon which the entire salvation narrative hinges.

Part of what made church such a powerful experience for me as a child and a young adult was that it was the one place where my own faults and failings were recognized and accepted, where people referred to themselves affectionately as "sinners," where it was taken as a given that the person standing in the pews beside you was morally fallible, but still you held hands and lifted your voice with hers as you worshipped in song. This camaraderie came from a collective understanding of evil—a belief that each person harbored within them a potential for sin and deserved, despite it, divine grace. It's this notion of shared fallibility that lent Hybels's 9/11 sermon its power, as he suggested that his own longing for revenge was only a difference of degree—not of kind—from the acts of the terrorists. And it's precisely this acknowledgement of collective guilt that makes it possible for a community to observe the core virtues of the faith: mercy, forgiveness, grace.

The irony is that, at a time when we are in need of potent metaphors to help us make sense of our darkest impulses, the church has chosen to remain silent on the problem of evil, for fear of becoming obsolete. The short-term advantages of such a strategy are as obvious as its ultimate futility. Like so many formerly oppositional institutions, the church is now becoming a symptom of the culture rather than an antidote to it, giving us one less place to turn for a sober counter-narrative to the simplistic story of moral progress that stretches from Silicon Valley to Madison Avenue. Hell may be an elastic concept, as varied as the thousands of malevolencies it has described throughout history, but it remains our most resilient metaphor for the evil both around and within us. True compassion is possible not because we are ignorant that life can be hell, but because we know that it can be.

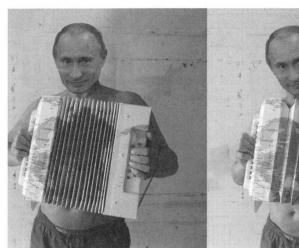

Yuri Solomko, *Geopolitical Accordion*, 2014
yurisolomko.com

PUTIN AND THE WEST

THE POLITICS OF EURASIANISM

by Brickey LeQuire

VLADIMIR PUTIN'S DISTRUST of Western-style democracy, his occasional nostalgia for Russia's glorious tsarist past, his recurring anger at the Communist leaders who allowed the Soviet Union to collapse in 1991, and his determination for Russia to be once more a world power—all this has never been a secret. That he would violate international law and act on his imperialist ambitions perforce, however, has come as a surprise to Western leaders, journalists and scholars, who now seek to explain Putin's Ukrainian gambit and anticipate his next move—both difficult tasks, without a clear view of his long game. For now, Putin's boldness seems to have bolstered his public support, but Russia's territorial gains in Ukraine have been comparatively modest and the ensuing Western sanctions costly. An outright war of even brief duration could ruin Russia's economy and its remaining credibility in the international community. Regarded only in the short term, then, his strategy seems inexplicably high-risk, low-reward. A *New York Times* op-ed from August offers the assessment that "Mr. Putin is not rational"; undeterred by the prospect of financial catastrophe to be followed, inevitably, by diminishing popularity, he remains a "smirking enigma."

Perhaps Putin is a megalomaniac myopically succumbing to his lust for power. But a more plausible explanation for Putin's recent decisions is that he is neither economically illiterate nor libidinously violent, but motivated instead by political commitments that we do not fully understand. Perhaps Russia's use of force in Ukraine is a means to an end determined by a set of values that differ from our own. In recent years, an anti-liberal, anti-Western political doctrine known as Eurasianism, or neo-Eurasianism, has gained popularity not only with Russian voters but also among some regime officials—and Putin's public statements clearly bespeak a degree of sympathy for Eurasianist thought. Those Western journalists who have discovered the Eurasianist agenda have suggested it as the direct explanation for Putin's actions in Ukraine, citing, in particular, the political theory of Aleksandr Dugin, one of Russia's most prominent public intellectuals.

Values matter in politics, and the leading role that Eurasian ideology now plays in Russian public discourse makes it imperative that we take it seriously as a potential cause, rather than merely a symptom, of the broader rightward shift in the region. At the same time, we should bear in mind that it is difficult to identify and impossible to predict an idea's actual influence on historic events. Without a clear portrait of Dugin's thought, it is hard to understand Putin's long-term strategy in Ukraine; but we should resist the urge to view Dugin as the secret key to that strategy. While Putin's philosophy is undoubtedly informed by Eurasianism, his promotion of the ideology's most extreme variants may provide cover for a more pragmatic agenda.

F OR CENTURIES, DEBATES about Russia's identity (cultural, political, geographical) have turned on the question of its relation to the West. Some voices emphasize economic ties and cultural commonalities with Europe; others focus on Russia's relations to its Eastern neighbors and its distinctive history as an Orthodox, Slavic and uniquely Eurasian power. Eurasianism as a political theory emerged from this second tradition early in the twentieth century and revived in the years following 1991. Dugin, a political scientist originally from Moscow, has shaped its modern development and remains its most noteworthy exponent.

A journalist during the final years of the Soviet Union, Dugin was co-founder of the National Bolshevik Party in 1994. He rose to prominence over the 1990s, cementing his reputation in 1997 with the book *Foundations of Geopolitics: The Geopolitical Future of Russia*, which was adopted as a textbook at many institutions, including the General Staff Academy of the Russian Armed Forces. In 1998 he was appointed advisor on geopolitics to Gennady Seleznev, who was then chairman of the Russian State Duma. By the time the 9/11 attacks suggested (to some) that America's days as a global military and economic superpower might be numbered, Dugin had made connections in the military, secret services and presidential administration as well. In 2002 he founded the Eurasia Party in Russia, and he continues to champion an international Eurasian movement as an active scholar and frequent news commentator. In 2008 he was given a prestigious academic post at Moscow State University, and his geopolitical theory has reportedly become the political creed of high officials in the present government, including Sergei Glazyev, Putin's senior advisor on Ukraine, who was one of the first seven Russian citizens targeted by American sanctions in March 2014. Dugin's university appointment ended in September of this year (the exact circumstances of his departure are contested), but there is little doubt that he still has the ear of the Russian people, including a number of its ruling elite.

On a practical level, Dugin calls for the political unification of the former Soviet republics as well as Mongolia, the Caucasus and "the eastern and northern shores of the Caspian." The strength of the envisioned Eurasia is to be supported internationally by diplomatic alliances along three "axes" radiating from Moscow to Berlin, Tokyo and Tehran. On questions of value, Dugin defines himself in opposition to modern liberalism, understood broadly as the ideology underlying the politics of individual rights, the global market economy and state sovereignty under the current system of international law. In 2009 Dugin published *The Fourth Political Theory* (English translation, 2012), which draws together his geopolitical theory, his syncretic anti-liberal ideology and his apocalyptic view of modern history and Russia's place in it.

As set out in that book, Dugin's vision of Eurasia, or Greater Russia, is rooted in the political thought of the German jurist Carl Schmitt (1888-1985). Schmitt—who feared the Russians almost as much as he loathed liberal democracy—argued that the national state with sovereignty over a determinate geographic territory is only one type of political entity among several. For Schmitt, political communities are ultimately defined not by law or geography but by the fundamental existential distinction between friend and enemy. A human group—a nation, a race, a religion, an economic class—truly becomes a political entity only when the "friendship" between its members is strong enough to motivate actual war (involving "the real possibility of physical killing") against a common enemy.

Dugin is not the first scholar since Schmitt to claim that the sovereign nation-state, originating in Reformation-era Europe and best exemplified by England and France, is not a universally applicable model. In 1936, Eric Voegelin—influenced by Schmitt's theory, although terrified by its practical implications—claimed that Austria was not yet a nation but existed precariously between "Reich" and "state." (His hope that an authoritarian government could suppress factionalism long enough for the Austrian people to develop a common political identity was disappointed two years later, when Nazi militants occupied public spaces and seized government buildings, and Austria was annexed by the German Reich, without military resistance.) Benedict Anderson's 1983 study *Imagined Communities* makes the case that nation-states are exactly that—imagined communities with historic origins in Western nationalism, particularly as it developed in the Americas and France. In 1992, Basil Davidson argued that many of Africa's social and political problems should be directly attributed to the imposition of national organization on tribal society during the era of decolonization.

Following a similar logic, Dugin contends that the "Westphalian system"— that is, "the existing order of sovereign nation-states and national sovereignty"— "no longer corresponds to the current global balance of powers. New actors of transnational and subnational scale are affirming their growing importance, and it is evident that the world is in need of a new paradigm in international relations." While Dugin suggests the "village-state" as a model of small-scale political organization, his real concern is with what Schmitt called a *Großraum* (literally "great space"). Schmitt believed that empires, rather than states, were fast becoming the main international agents, and that an empire, along with the smaller states within its sphere of influence, constituted a larger spatial order with a loose but nevertheless common political identity. The Western Hemisphere under the Monroe Doctrine (Schmitt's example) and today's European Union are *Großräume*; a unified Eurasia ruled by a renewed Russian empire would be another.

In part, the argument for *Großräume* rests on the idea that in international relations, as in economics, bigger is better; collective action is more effective on a larger scale. But it also depends on the claim that transnational political entities can and do exist. Dugin understands the *civilization*, rather than the nation-state, "as the foundational subject, pole and actor of contemporary world politics." He deconstructs the nineteenth-century European concept of "civilization" as the historical process by which "culture" in the abstract progressively triumphs over barbarism. "Civilization in the context of the twenty-first century signifies precisely this: a zone of the steady and rooted influence of a definite social-cultural style, most often (though not necessarily) coinciding with the borders of the diffusion of the world religions." Following Samuel Huntington, Dugin lists as examples the Western, Confucian, Japanese, Islamic, Indian, Slavic-Orthodox, Latin American and (possibly) African civilizations, though with the qualification that Western civilization is politically fragmented into two or more "large spaces."

Civilizations are not abstractions but actual groupings of people with common histories and values—and enemies. Their distinct interests and diverse political cultures persist, notwithstanding Francis Fukuyama's argument that liberal democracy represents the "end point of mankind's ideological evolution" and the "final form of human government," or that worldwide consensus as to its legitimacy would lead to what Alexandre Kojève called the "universal and homogeneous state." At least, this is what Dugin and his allies hope that history will demonstrate. At present, in Dugin's apocalyptic view, it seems Fukuyama's prophecies have come true.

THE TITLE OF *The Fourth Political Theory* refers not to a theoretical position Dugin has developed but to an ideology that has still to be created, not in thought but through collective action. The modern world has so far been shaped by three successive political theories—liberalism, fascism and communism. By the end of the twentieth century, following the collapse of European fascism in 1945, and Soviet communism in 1991, liberalism had won out over rival ideologies and begun remaking the world in its own image, creating a grim condition Dugin calls "postmodernity": "the glorification of total freedom and the independence of the individual from any kind of limits, including reason, morality, identity (social, ethnic, or even gender), discipline, and so on." Victorious liberalism destroys the traditional family and existing political societies, replacing them with a universal economic order: "Fukuyama's 'end of history' arrives, economics in the form of the global capitalist market, replaces politics, and states and nations are dissolved in the melting pot of world globalization." The ensuing homogeneity leads to domination on an unprecedented scale: "Humanity under liberalism, comprised entirely of individuals, is naturally drawn toward universality and seeks to become global and unified. Thus, the projects of 'world government' or globalism are born."

To forge a "fourth political theory" that can overcome liberalism is neither an individual nor an academic task—it is a question of collective political will; and for Russia "it is a matter of life or death—'to be or not to be'":

> If Russia chooses "to be," then it will automatically bring about the creation of a Fourth Political Theory. Otherwise, for Russia there remains only the choice "not to be," which will mean to quietly leave the historical and world stage, dissolving into a global order which is not created or governed by us.

The ontology that underlies Dugin's neo-Eurasianism comes from his reading of the German philosopher Martin Heidegger, who, like Schmitt, publicly condoned National Socialism while Hitler was in power and never subsequently expressed regret for his complicity in the Nazi horrors. Heidegger used the word *Dasein* to refer to human existence. *Dasein*, in Dugin's interpretation, is not

Yuri Solomko, *Cossack Mamay*, 2014

the existence of an individual human being; it is the collective being of a group living a shared way of life. Unlike liberal political theory, which begins with a concept of the individual person and his or her needs and rights, the "fourth political theory" presupposes *Dasein* as the fundamental and most important unit in politics (and so privileges the collective over the individual). Russian *Dasein* is, historically, the political existence of an imperial people; if the citizens of the Russian Federation acquiesce to mere nation-state status, then Russia itself will have ceased to be. To succumb to the processes of Americanizing globalization would be to commit civilizational suicide.

Moscow is essential to the Eurasianist project, for it is an avowedly imperial enterprise to be carried out under Russian political leadership and through the influence of Russian culture. Imperialism is fundamental to Russian identity, Dugin argues, but it is also, simultaneously, a form of humanitarianism. Russian civilization is unique, and the Russian people are the messianic representatives not only of other ethnic groups within their sphere of influence but also of all peoples who are oppressed or disadvantaged by Western hegemony. Imperial expansion is understood not as the self-interested conquest of inferiors but as the self-sacrificial liberation of equals in a worldwide crusade against liberalism.

Dugin's political project is to gain explicit recognition for the political existence of "Slavic-Orthodox" civilization via the creation of a transnational *Großraum* under Russian leadership. It is part of a broader theoretical vision for a "multipolar" world of autonomous Great Powers, with clear implications for international law. It stands in opposition to the universal order of sovereign nation-states created by the architects of the United Nations. More specifically, it is incompatible with the national sovereignty of Ukraine as declared by its parliament in 1990, and as recognized by the Russian Federation in 1994. As Dugin puts it, "The Western border of the Eurasianist civilization goes somewhat more East of the Western border of Ukraine, making that newly-formulated government *a fortiori* fragile and not viable."

Whether "Slavic-Orthodox" civilization has a political future remains to be seen, but Vladimir Putin's actions in Ukraine are certainly congruent with Dugin's political agenda. Not only are they effectively redrawing the map of Eastern Europe along Eurasianist lines, but they are also rooted in a similar view of Russian identity: "The Russian people are state-builders, as evidenced by the existence of Russia. Their great mission is to unite and bind together a civilization." The annexation of the Crimean peninsula was thus entirely consonant with the neo-Eurasianist agenda. Its de jure authorization by popular referendum may have been an attempt to comply formally, albeit retroactively, with the principles of national sovereignty and self-determination, foundational norms of the modern international legal order enshrined in the UN Charter.

However, with the Republic of Crimea and the federal city of Sevastopol safely incorporated into the Russian Federation, and much of eastern Ukraine likely to follow, Putin's disregard for international law has gone from patent to overt. He has ordered Russian military and intelligence operations within another sovereign nation's borders; more importantly, he has asserted the right to do so, unilaterally, anywhere that Russian-speaking people stand in need of protection.

Further, Putin's government is arguably taking concrete steps toward the creation of an institutional order in the former Soviet space, and toward the integration of new groups into the politically organized portion of Russian civilization. In 2010, Russia, Belarus and Kazakhstan created the Eurasian Customs Union, which lifted customs controls over goods crossing member states' borders in July 2011. Beginning in January 2012, the common customs area became a common market—the Common Economic Space (CES) of Russia, Belarus and Kazakhstan. In October 2011, Putin announced a plan, which will go into effect in January 2015, for Russia and its neighbors to forge a Eurasian Union, "a powerful supranational association capable of becoming one of the poles in the modern world." Economic integration will proceed quickly, Putin claims, because knowledge of "the experience of the E.U. and other regional associations ... means we are in a position to avoid mistakes and unnecessary bureaucratic superstructures." Political dimensions of the integration project are manifest as well. In the future, the CES framework "will also include common visa and migration policies, allowing border controls between our states to be lifted."

The question whether Russia stands on the "wrong side of history," as President Obama has repeatedly insisted, has yet to be decided. In Putin's view, the answer depends not (as Obama presumes) on its compliance with international law but on the success or failure of the present integration project:

> I am convinced that the establishment of the Eurasian Union and efficient integration are approaches that will enable members to take a prominent place in our complicated, twenty-first-century world. Only by standing together will all our countries be able to take their places as leaders of global growth and drivers of progress, only together will they succeed and prosper.

So far, Armenia, Kyrgyzstan and Tajikistan have expressed interest in joining the original CES states. More members are wanted, though no one will be forced to join: "The Eurasian Union is an open project. We welcome other partners to it, particularly CIS member states. At the same time, we are not going to hurry up or nudge anyone. A state must only join on its sovereign decision based on its long-term national interests." To question Putin's sincerity would be to miss the point; to discount his sanguinity would be foolhardy. In recent years not only Ukrainians, but Georgians and Moldovans as well, seem to be increasingly persuaded that their long-term interests lie in an alliance with Moscow.

THUS FAR, THEN, it seems that Putin's military interventions in Ukraine, his rhetorical justifications for them and his long-term political goals express a Eurasianist view of Russia's future. However, Putin and Dugin have differing views of how this Eurasian unification is to be accomplished and what the ultimate raison d'être of the Union will be—differences that may prove to be crucial.

Dugin follows Schmitt, for whom "all political concepts, images, and terms have a polemical meaning." On this way of thinking, only by defining itself against an enemy does a political grouping come into existence. His Eurasia will coalesce politically in reaction to Western cultural and economic (and military) aggression; Russia's legitimate preeminence will rest on its national identity as the West's foremost enemy. In fact, for Dugin, "the entirety of Russian history is a dialectical argument with the West and against Western culture, the struggle for upholding our own ... *Russian* truth, our own messianic idea, and our own version of the 'end of history,' no matter how it is expressed—through Muscovite Orthodoxy, Peter's secular empire, or the global Communist revolution." Amid the evils of global "postmodernity," to uphold Russian truth means to oppose the United States, which Dugin regards as the Antichrist, the representative and defender of a modern West that has "rejected the values of God and Tradition."

Here Dugin draws not only on Schmitt, a Roman Catholic who nostalgically described the medieval Christian empire as the restrainer of the Antichrist and the end the world, but also on a specifically Russian tradition of regarding Western threats in a political-theological light. In the opening paragraph of Tolstoy's *War and Peace*, for instance, someone exclaims, "I really believe [Napoleon Bonaparte] is Antichrist"—a view subsequently adopted by Pierre Bezukhov, the novel's hero. Tolstoy's own view may be more nuanced, but Dugin unambiguously identifies the United States as humanity's eschatological antagonist. The claim is to be taken literally: "This is not simply a metaphor capable of mobilizing the masses, but a religious fact of the Apocalypse." Russia's role in the Eurasianist project is not merely to secure political autonomy for the region, but to save it from the Western, the secular, the modern way of life. "Only a global crusade against the U.S., the West, globalization, and their political-ideological

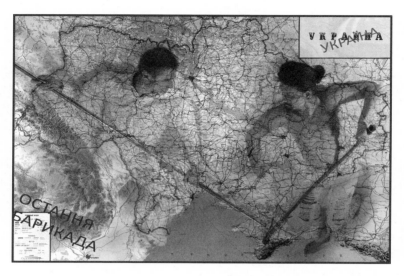

Yuri Solomko, *Last Barricade*, 2014

expression, liberalism, is capable of becoming an adequate response." In Dugin's view, Eurasianists stand in common cause with Hugo Chávez and Al Qaeda.

Many Western observers of this year's unrest in Ukraine know little or nothing of Dugin and fail to take Eurasianism seriously if they consider it at all. The *Economist*, for instance, lampooned Putin's promise to protect Russian speakers in other nations as "linguistic imperialism," illustrated with an amusing political map of the world as redrawn along linguistic, rather than national lines. (No mention was made of this map's striking similarity to Dugin's cartographic illustration of "The Eurasist Vision.") But journalists and some scholars who have taken note of Dugin's ideas have often made the opposite error, assuming that Putin's plans and motivation can be completely explained by them.

Timothy Snyder, for instance, writing for the *New York Review of Books*, argues on the basis of Dugin's writings that the Eurasian Union is an enemy of the West in ideological as well as strategic terms. Whereas the European Union's foundational commitment to universal human rights reflects wisdom hard-won through the nightmares of totalitarianism, the Eurasian Union will stand on a hodgepodge of the very fascist and Stalinist sentiments that led to the catastrophe of World War II. According to Anton Barbashin and Hannah Thoburn, writing in *Foreign Affairs*, Dugin is "Putin's Brain," and neo-Eurasianism the "Philosophy Behind Putin's Invasion of Crimea." Most dramatically—and as close as it comes to a response in kind—Robert Zubrin writes in the *National Review Online*:

> In short, Dugin's Eurasianism is a satanic cult. This is the ideology behind the Putin regime's "Eurasian Union" project. It is to this dark program, which threatens not only the prospects for freedom in Ukraine and Russia, but the peace of the world, that former Ukrainian president Victor Yanukovych tried to sell "his" country. It is against this program that the courageous protesters in the Maidan took their stand and—with scandalously little help from the West—somehow miraculously prevailed. It is on behalf of this program that the Putin regime has created a bloodbath in eastern Ukraine, which, following Dugin, it now terms "New Russia."

From this perspective, the conflict in Ukraine is not a quarrel over real estate but the clash of radically opposed belief systems and ways of life. If Putin's ultimate goal in Ukraine is the realization of Dugin's "fourth political theory," then both the most hawkish of American conservatives and the most outraged of liberals have it right. We are already at war with an enemy whose God-given goal is our annihilation. And Putin is an outright fascist with a principled disregard for universal human rights. His success would constitute a threat to freedom not only in Russia but also to its neighbors and, by extension, to the values of the international community.

As tempting as it is to view Dugin as the mastermind behind Putin's foreign policy, however, sober analysis suggests a more nuanced relationship between Dugin's neo-Eurasian ideology and Putin's efforts toward Eurasian political integration. Without a doubt, Putin profits from Dugin's ideological, anti-Western Eurasianist stance, to the extent that it stirs up public support for his regime. Perhaps it even sets some of the parameters for his policy. But there are clear signs that he does not entirely share it. Putin's Eurasianism is political, not ideological, and it seems likely that his current alliance with Dugin and company is strategic rather than heartfelt.

If Putin's recent actions were the product of neo-Eurasianist value commitments, then we could predict that Putin's future decisions in the region would be oriented toward the political formation of a Eurasian state, even at considerable expense to the existing Russian Federation's interests, *and*, further, that this task of state formation would be merely preparatory to the ultimate, morally imperative struggle against the United States and the broader Western commitment to free markets and individual human rights. It is worth noting that this prognosis does not correspond to Dugin's interpretation of events. Dugin considers Putin a patriotic pragmatist: "Intuitively striving to preserve and consolidate Russian sovereignty," he has written, "Putin entered into a conflict with the liberal West and its plans for globalization, but without forming his actions into an alternative ideology." Putin, for all his anti-Western rhetoric, sees no ideological clash between Europe and Eurasia. In a 2011 article announcing the formation of the Eurasian Union, he emphasized the similarity of their fundamental ideological commitments:

> In this respect, I would like to touch upon an important issue. Some of our neighbors explain their lack of interest in joining forward-looking integration projects in the post-Soviet space by saying that these projects contradict their pro-European stance. I believe that this is a false antithesis. We do not intend to cut ourselves off, nor do we plan to stand in opposition to anyone. The Eurasian Union will be based on universal integration principles as an essential part of Greater Europe united by shared values of freedom, democracy, and market laws.

If Putin does not understand democracy exactly as Westerners do, neither does he paint liberalism and those who adhere to it as a force of world-historical evil to be swept away in a coming apocalypse. It is worth keeping in mind that Putin could, after all, unleash a nuclear doomsday, should he so choose. His restraint

ОГЛЯДОВА КАРТА
УКРАЇНИ

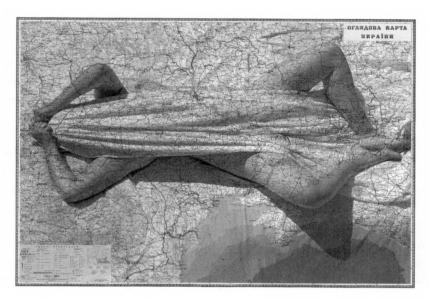

Yuri Solomko, *Ukraine*, 2009

in this matter deserves no special praise, perhaps, but in an era when a reactionary activist like Dugin has so many enthusiastic disciples, it isn't to be taken for granted.

More importantly, though, it might be worth asking why the Western press has been so eager to depict Putin's course of action in Ukraine as the direct outgrowth of either economic short-sightedness or an extremist anti-modern ideology, rather than as the prudential calculations of a hard-nosed, experienced student of international affairs. Dugin does indeed loom large in Russian public life, not least because he enjoys the seemingly constant favor of the mainstream news media—particularly television, over which the Kremlin exercises near-complete control. Barbashin and Thoburn argue that Dugin's outsize media presence is a sign that Putin approves his message; logically, however, all we can infer from the evidence is that Putin wants Dugin in the limelight.

Why? That is the question. It is difficult to take Dugin seriously as a political theorist, but he is right to note that Shakespeare's *Hamlet* is a political drama. Its protagonist's famed existential question is not posed in the abstract. When finally he makes his belated decision, it is by giving the lie to his usurping uncle: "This is I, Hamlet the Dane." The true prince is not an individual—he is Denmark. Yet he lived to dither for so long by putting on "an antic disposition," pretending to be mad out of grief, or love, or an academician's preoccupation with words, words, words. Half a year after the *Anschluss* of Crimea, those who deem Putin irrational or insane all agree with Claudius: "Madness in great ones must not unwatched go." They should also heed the observation of Polonius: "Though this be madness, yet there is method in't." It is possible that Dugin's intellectual antics receive so much tacit approval from the Russian government—and, accordingly, so much attention from Western readers—precisely because they are theoretical flights of fancy with little direct influence on government policy. It would be rash to ignore Dugin on the basis of this conjecture. But to allow Dugin's ideological Eurasianism to distract us from Putin's pragmatic efforts to bring the Eurasian Union into political existence would, indeed, be madness.

Obviously, we who have ignored Russia since the end of the Cold War have much to learn. A good place to start would be with the recognition that Eurasianism, like Americanism, exists in diverse forms, and the distinctions between them matter a great deal. The more disturbing Dugin's neo-Eurasianism becomes, the more Putin appears not as a sworn enemy of the West so much as a practically minded protector of his own constituency—defined not under (current) international law as the citizens and nationals of the existing Russian Federation but according to his own conception of an ethnic people with the historic responsibility of building a politically organized, multi-ethnic civilization.

At the same time, of course, we should acknowledge that even the more moderate, pragmatic forms of Eurasianism are indeed at odds with the (broadly speaking) liberal and democratic values that reign in North America and Western Europe, and that there is probably precious little we can do to impose these values even on Donbas, much less the vast reaches of Eurasia. It is discomfiting to think that Putin may be in the thrall of neo-Eurasianist dogma, but perhaps even more sobering to acknowledge that he isn't—that his actions may be the result of entirely rational decisions calculated to make Greater Russia a political reality, to the Russian people's long-term advantage, if not to ours.

Lutz Bacher, *The Lee Harvey Oswald Interview*, 2013
Courtesy of the artist and the Portikus Gallery

THE EXILE'S GAME

DUCHAMP, MODERNISM AND THE ART OF CHESS

by Thomas Chatterton Williams

STEFAN ZWEIG'S 1942 novella, *Chess Story*, set on a steamer headed from New York to Buenos Aires, recounts the tale of a Viennese lawyer, Dr. B., who had been imprisoned by Nazis and subjected to an extreme form of mental violence. Held in a hotel room in total isolation for one year, with nothing to distract himself—no pens, paper, cigarettes or even a wristwatch to mark the days—he was thrust into "a completely timeless and dimensionless void." It was a punishment meant to break a man as surely as the rack, yet Dr. B. managed to preserve his sanity, he explains one night to an intrigued passenger, by pilfering a book of nothing more than 150 master-level chess games. There were no accompanying illustrations, but he nonetheless proceeded to lose himself in the notations of these concluded matches, memorizing the variations and replaying them on his checkered bedspread, until one day he found he no longer needed the book or the squares and could simply shut his eyes and visualize the pieces on the board, separating his mind into opposing armies of black and white, ferociously attempting to mate himself even as he deftly avoided being mated. He stopped sleeping and focused all his energy on searching for the right move. The psychological toll of this "chess sickness," as he later calls it, had caused Dr. B. to suffer a breakdown. When he recovered and was finally freed, he didn't dare go near a chessboard again, until it came to his attention that the reigning world champion, an idiot savant named Czentovic, was onboard the same ocean liner. Dr. B. sits down and defeats him, before making a fatal error in the rematch and slipping back into madness.

Marveling at the thought of such single-minded obsessives, the narrator of the story, himself an amateur, reflects:

> The more I now sought to form an impression of such a temperament,
> the more unimaginable appeared to me a mind absorbed for a lifetime in

a domain of sixty-four black and white squares. From my own experience I was well aware of the mysterious attraction of the "royal game," which, alone among the games devised by man, regally eschews the tyranny of chance and awards its palms of victory only to the intellect, or rather to a certain type of intellectual gift. But is it not already an insult to call chess anything so narrow as a game?

In real life, perhaps no figure in recent memory so exemplified the idea of "chess sickness"—that insatiable need to find the right move at the cost of everything else—as the pioneering French artist Marcel Duchamp. The father of Dada and inspiration to the Surrealists, Duchamp was, by the end of his life in the late 1960s, widely considered one of the finest, most original minds in twentieth-century art, alongside Picasso and a handful of others. He achieved immense renown (and even infamy) for for his 1913 painting *Nude Descending a Staircase*, the practically unclassifiable *The Bride Stripped Bare by Her Bachelors, Even (The Large Glass)*, and the groundbreaking readymade sculptures that for better or worse provided a preview for so much contemporary art. Nonetheless, he essentially turned his back on painting, complaining that "after ten years ... I was bored with it. ... From 1912 on I decided to stop being a painter in the professional sense." Instead, he tried "to look for another personal way." "Of course," he acknowledged, "I couldn't expect anyone to be interested in what I was doing."

By the 1920s, when he was in his early thirties, Duchamp seems to have found this more personal way forward. A large part of what was so frustrating and uninteresting about modern painting, in his view, was its overly aesthetic, "retinal" nature: the inherent superficiality of visual representation. Duchamp was foremost an ideas man, for whom a work of art needed to accomplish significantly more than to please the eye. According to his biographer Calvin Tomkins, he was increasingly driven to "make visible a 'nonperceptible' experience"—in other words, to render states of mind manifest. Two paintings he completed during a short stint in Munich, with their emphasis on inside jokes and what he preposterously referred to as "eroticism," were a turning point. And it was while working on these nonrepresentational but not quite abstract—and still meticulously painted—canvases that he began to conceive his enigmatic masterpiece *The Large Glass*. Constructed from two large panes of glass with various materials inserted between them, it is less a painting than a humorous, pseudoscientific gesture at the hidden psychological forces and urges that animate our libidos. At least that is one take on this "picture," which in no way resembles the wedding party invoked by its title, and which required Duchamp to concoct a new physics and mathematics to convey its inner "laws." (His copious notes, published as *The Green Box*, only further complicate the work's meaning.)

Whether *The Large Glass* is the most important artwork of the last century or a complete hoax—these are open questions—Duchamp claimed, during the eight years it took to complete it, to have lost interest in the artistic process so completely that he left the work "definitively unfinished." (When the glass panels were cracked in transport, he even noted approvingly that this had been an improvement.) Having gone as far as he could with fine art as a means of conveying pure ideas, and relentlessly searching for a way to create without filters, the lifelong amateur began dedicating himself to the game of chess. Indeed, he became a full-fledged slave to the 64 squares. In a letter back home to France from New York, where he lived after the War, he acknowledged that "the only thing that could interest me now is a potion that would make me play chess *divinely*."

So dedicated was Duchamp to this pursuit, Tomkins reports, that on his 1927 honeymoon in the south of France he "was mostly absent, playing in a chess tournament in Nice that he had entered as a warm-up for the French championships, which were being held the next month in Chamonix." At night he would stay up studying chess problems, frustrating his fiancée Lydie to the point that, according to Man Ray, one day she glued all of the pieces to his board. Incredibly, this was not some quixotic vanity project on Duchamp's part—he achieved the equivalent of a master-level command of the game, played on the national team alongside Alekhine, the world champion at the time, and was ultimately considered by many to be one of the finest players in France in his day.

This improbable, practically monastic midlife pivot away from the demands and rewards of artistic production and toward the cerebral pleasures of this insular game both mirrored and anticipated the progression of modern art—the impulse being always to strip down and arrive at what is most essential. "Reduce, reduce, reduce was my thought," he explained years later. "But at the same time my aim was turning inward, rather than toward externals. And later, following this view, I came to feel that an artist might use anything—a dot, a line, the most conventional or unconventional symbol—to say what he wanted to say."

Duchamp's sudden turn to chess might be seen as nothing more than this modernist impulse taken to its logical extreme. Though in the popular imagination we tend to think of the game of chess, when taken as a serious pursuit, as the domain of extreme nerds of the Bobby Fischer mold, in the figure of Duchamp we can see something much more romantic and daring at work. Chess, far from being some dry or merely scientific hobby, becomes a legitimate artistic endeavor in its own right—and perhaps even a purer creative expression than all of the rest. Duchamp seemed to conclude as much: "Not all artists are chess players," he famously quipped, "but all chess players are artists."

Lutz Bacher, *The Lee Harvey Oswald Interview*, 2013

But if chess players are artists, who is their audience? One of the great ironies of early modern art, as Tomkins points out, was that "in trying to break down the traditional barriers between artist and viewer—and, by implication, between art and life—advanced artists alienated a large part of the public." This was especially true in painting and the visual arts, but also evident in jazz music, literature and, perhaps most obviously, the post-Bauhaus and Corbusier aesthetic that dominated twentieth-century architecture and design. The flip side to this alienation was supposed to be a deeper and more fruitful interaction with the rare audiences capable of involving themselves as spectator-partners in the creative process—an aspiration that became "an essential element of Duchamp's thinking from 1912 on." In chess, this aspiration is taken to an almost absurd extreme: one's opponent becomes the sole intelligent spectator-consumer of one's imaginative output.

And the game itself becomes the absolute reduction of the artwork to the most elemental means of creative expression—a complex, fleeting and hermetic procession of elegant thoughts.

"**M**UCH OF AN exile's life is taken up with compensating for disorienting loss by creating a new world to rule," wrote Edward Said. "It is not surprising that so many exiles seem to be novelists [and] chess players." A little over three years ago, I moved from New York City, where I had just started a novel, to Paris. I didn't come for studies or a job; I simply moved here with my wife, who is French, because she had a work opportunity and we were both vaguely aware that it would be easier to start a family in France than in New York. But it wasn't so calculated as that: we were freshly married and in love and the idea of moving to Paris, her hometown and a city I had often visited and adored, didn't require a tremendous amount of analysis. We quickly packed up our apartment in Brooklyn and shipped it overseas. Within a few weeks I was back sitting at my dining room table working on my manuscript; only the slant of the light outside my window had changed—at least initially that's how it seemed to me.

I have come to think a lot about Duchamp and his unencumbered style of living and creating during these past few years. Such an example seems especially apposite now that I find myself in my thirties, an immigrant in a foreign land, consumed by a prolonged struggle to convert ideas into that precarious thing "art," and slipping deeper into my own prolonged periods of what I can only call a comparatively-mild-to-at-times-rather-intense strain of chess sickness. During these days away from home, I have occupied both of the introverted roles Said

MAN IN THE MOON
ESSAYS ON FATHERS & FATHERHOOD
edited by Stephanie G'Schwind

"Science claims it will one day be able to eliminate fathers from the equation by mating bone marrow with ovum. When that day comes, I imagine this book, along with a handful of other works (*King Lear, Fun Home*) will become even more necessary. Herein find the blueprints for the mystery, the maps for the uncharted, the keys to the archetype."—**Nick Flynn**

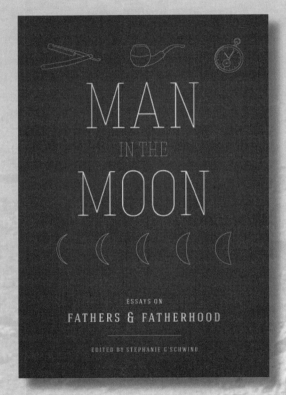

Drawing from among the country's leading literary journals and publications, *Man in the Moon* gathers essays in which sons, daughters, and fathers explore the elusive nature of this intimate relationship and find unique ways to frame and understand it: through astronomy, arachnology, storytelling, map-reading, television, puzzles, DNA, and so on. At turns painfully familiar, comic, and heartbreaking, the works in this collection also deliver moments of searing beauty and hard-earned wisdom.

Essays by Dan Beachy-Quick, Robin Black, Bill Capossere, Matthew Ferrence, Carole Firstman, Gina Frangello, Debra Gwartney, Jim Kennedy, Joan Marcus, Neil Mathison, Richard McCann, Dinty W. Moore, Donna George Storey, Deborah Thompson, Jerald Walker, Thomas White, & Brendan Wolfe

Published by the Center for Literary Publishing
Distributed by the University Press of Colorado
www.upcolorado.com

mentions, though neither pursuit is new. I had published a book (albeit a memoir) before leaving, and I grew up locked in mental combat with my father—a scholarly chess autodidact who will forever be for me the *other* emblem of the game's Sisyphean struggle.

Whatever else one does, one does not readily elude one's father. And however much my adult interest in chess follows the example set by Duchamp, I am still constructing my proverbial game in relation to his. Pappy is in his late seventies now and remains a formidable opponent, though he never joined clubs or sought to play competitively. He's far too solitary for that. And unorthodox—*he only ever wants to use black.* I suspect this is because even in make-believe he would rather not allow himself to forget that his starting position has been a comparatively disadvantageous one. (This insistence on beginning behind only seems to reinforce his deeply American can-do belief that despite—or maybe even because of—the riskier opening, victory always remains a possibility; as a result, he refuses to concede even practically irreversible positions and has salvaged more than a few of them.) In any event, it is certainly the case that he has spent his entire life in exile (in the fullest sense of the word) in his own country—most notably as a Southerner fleeing Jim Crow, first for the West and then the Northeast, and as a black man surfacing in social and professional spaces almost always devoid of similar faces.

When they were living in Santa Monica in the Seventies, my mother tells me, Pappy would often pass the evening hours hunched over his chessboard with their taciturn neighbor, a Russian émigré my parents referred to, descriptively enough, as "Rudy the Russian." The two men scarcely spoke—they didn't need to. Rudy would knock after work, they'd shake hands with formality and then together they would dissolve into those familiar checkered squares. I had not thought of this before, but now that I do, I am positive that both of these men were using the game as Said suggests—to gain entry into some other dimension beyond the absurdity of their respective heres and nows, to that place where things would be compelled to make logical sense. I am not that kind of exile, then, not at all. But for what it's worth, I am often looking for some clarity and, perhaps more than that, a little silence too.

"Chess is a school of silence," Duchamp once reminded a puzzled interviewer. What a wonderful phrase. I couldn't count the number of times a day that—even as my grasp of French progresses—I am tongue-tied, at an agonizing loss for basic words, or worse, beset by the nightmarish sensation of being some hapless dog, chasing the tail end of conversations I can tantalizingly envision but will never quite grasp. And yet there is rarely any genuine quiet to be had here, just a continuous rush of semi-intelligible background noise. It is no coincidence that it wasn't until I found myself far from family and friends and the comfort of ambient English—which is to say, far from a fully legible world—that my lifelong interest in the game metastasized into full-on chess fever. I wouldn't be able to pinpoint when precisely this transition began, were it not for Chess. com's impressive record-keeping features. A quick search as I write this reveals that, since joining on April 22, 2012, I have clocked some 8,691 games of five- and ten-minute "live blitz" on my main account alone. (I have several.)

FOR LARGE SWATHS of the past two years, then, I have found myself enthralled by this game for two, four, five, six, sometimes even eight hours a day, the time flitting past not in increments of seconds, minutes or even whole nights and days, but as a series of opening, middle- and end-game scenarios to be solved. The sheer fecundity of the internet, the inexhaustible supply of skilled partners from Singapore to Malta, the YouTube video tutorials and those Borgesian über-libraries of past games scrupulously archived and indexed, have all conspired to facilitate a level of chess binging that Duchamp could only dream of and that would absolutely shatter Dr. B.

I began visiting this world with such regularity and insistence that it struck my wife as a problem of some gravity. But what she observed was only the half of it. I was surreptitiously conjuring the board with my third eye while standing in line at the grocery store, while falling asleep, and increasingly even while I was sitting at the table, purportedly writing. There is a particular, deeply satisfying game with black that comes up rarely but with a reliable consistency, which I am perpetually on the lookout for. Once played, it can take cycling through three- or four-dozen games to encounter it again. The situation is as follows: Black opens with a Latvian Gambit—pawn e4, pawn f4—in response to White opening with pawn e4, knight f3. In so doing, Black invites White to ransack his king's side for material advantage. If White too aggressively takes the bait, however—which is not uncommon—there is a line of play in which Black further sacrifices a rook to White's invading knight to achieve a cunning bishop attack on White's queen. As White scampers to protect its most valuable piece, the attack progresses by way of a subtle undisclosed check from Black's queen (seemingly defensively positioned) on e1. White will make several more attempts, in vain, to evade check and save its queen, but the latter has been irretrievably lost for several moves now, usually unbeknownst to White. After the queen falls, checkmate or resignation happens very swiftly.

It is a stunningly gorgeous and powerfully counterintuitive trap, one that has transfixed me and taken on a kind of metaphorical symbolism in my mind

Lutz Bacher, *The Lee Harvey Oswald Interview*, 2013

for the idea of noble abandonment. Perhaps it is even an image of the writing life itself, which after all is always premised upon tremendous initial risk in the hope of some nebulous future payoff. Here I am, three years into a novel that has required no small amount of material sacrifice and yet, at this point, exists solely in a Microsoft Word document and in a corner of my mind—which is to say, exists solely as a *strategy*. And the lesson that these hundreds, if not thousands, of Latvian games I've played through have taught me is that Black can also lose. There are many ways for that to happen, even in the best-laid scenario.

O N DAYS WHEN the correct word eludes me, when I find myself deleting entire scenes and chapters and starting over from a blank, when I find myself in this still-foreign land where the sockets in the walls do not accommodate all of my plugs, where I still do not speak the language fluently and am still searching for order and quiet, on days when I cannot help wondering whether I will ever finish this manuscript or whether I have already sacrificed too many valuable pieces for a relatively tenuous position, I open my browser and seek refuge in those squares and in that perfect calm. Only there, as Duchamp observed:

> It's complete. There are no bizarre conclusions like in art, where you have all kinds of reasonings and conclusions. It's absolutely clear-cut. It's a marvelous piece of Cartesianism. And so imaginative that it doesn't even look Cartesian at first. The beautiful combinations that people invent in chess are only Cartesian after they are explained. And yet when it's explained there is no mystery. It's a pure logical conclusion, and it cannot be refuted.

Of course, there remains the question of whether an artist ought to idealize this kind of "Cartesianism" or try to challenge it. Art, in the fundamentally Tolstoyan sense my exiled father reared me to conceive of it, would bear scant resemblance to disinterested philosophical investigation; rather, aesthetic values are determined by moral ones and must serve some larger purpose, addressing ethical, metaphysical—or at least social—issues in order to help real human beings understand how best to live, or how best to live *better*. A lifelong admirer of Maimonides, Pappy would have literature—would have all creative output— function as one more entry in the necessary and ever-expanding guide for the perplexed.

Chess by comparison would seem a selfish and lonesome pursuit. Indeed, so would most Duchampian art. Duchamp "had no affinity for social causes or for any view of art as a direct expression of personal emotions or communal yearnings," notes Tomkins. In his own words, "Art is like a shipwreck ... it's every man for himself." Which is why chess, an utterly disengaged mental exercise, could come to represent the best possible kind of art for Duchamp—the figure who perhaps more than any other functions as the progenitor and prophet of our received aesthetic preferences. In the wake of modernism and all the subsequent permutations and movements, it has become rote to accept Duchamp's conclusions almost *prima facie*. Indeed, there have not been many major artists (of any discipline) since Tolstoy to earnestly espouse the moral imperative of art over the modernist one.

Perhaps it sounds naïve and sappy, but there seems to be a certain perversity, or at least a distinct lack of courage, embedded in the impulse to reduce the entire forest of art to a singular, recondite tree—tempting as such a delimitation may be when struggling to encompass the multitude. With this in mind, not so unlike Dr. B., I find myself having to guard against overexposure to the board. Far from moving on a continuum, my own creative life has become a divided one: the private pleasures of the chessboard a temptation I must actively counterbalance with a sustained effort to engage, however vainly and ineptly, the world beyond these 64 fixed-yet-unlimited squares.

And yet isn't there always an incongruity between intent and result? Duchamp's great achievement—indeed what, despite his claims, makes his work worthy of even my father's esteem—cannot be found in the particular pieces he made or in the records of games that he played (though some of both were great). Rather, it is a byproduct of the fact that he managed simultaneously to excavate a measure of transcendence in the familiar (a bathroom fixture, a bicycle wheel, a board game) and in turn to render familiar the transcendent—showing us that even if no one else sees it, art is, or certainly can be, encountered everywhere around and even inside us. In that way, then, it is indeed a lot like the game of chess: both are aspects of the same indispensable philosophy of survival.

Danilo Santinelli, *Childhood*, 2013

FOES OF GOD

DON DELILLO'S COSMOPOLIS

by Ben Jeffery

IT WOULDN'T BE absurd to describe Don DeLillo's *Cosmopolis* as the most prescient American novel of the last fifteen years. Published in 2003, it's a slim and strangely told story about capitalism, the thirteenth book of DeLillo's career and—so far—the only one to have been made into a film.* When it first appeared, critics chalked it up as a late-career curiosity or, more often, tore it apart for being pretentious and stale. In one of two acidic reviews published by the *New York Times*, Walter Kirn described it as "a numbing abacus calculation in prose," while in the other Michiko Kakutani called it "a major dud" and "hopelessly clichéd." In my own opinion, verdicts like these are a lot stupider than anything in DeLillo's novel, but there's no denying that *Cosmopolis* is an awkward book with some significant flaws. None of its characters are life-like. The dialogue, which is heavily stylized, can be hard going at times and occasionally feels like it's meant to be satire without actually being funny (an odd quality that comes out all the more in Cronenberg's movie). There are a couple of embarrassing forays into rap music and nightclubbing, lead-footed jokes, unconvincing set pieces and a long-winded and very obscure final scene. Those problems don't spoil the experience, but they do make *Cosmopolis* feel less substantial than, say, *White Noise* (1985) or *Libra* (1988), the heavyweight triumphs of DeLillo's career.

For all of that, *Cosmopolis* is an authentically strange achievement: a mostly forgotten minor novel that's also a suitably murky conclusion to the story DeLillo's been telling about America for the last half-century. I've come to think that it is a deeply political book, one that raises a series of pertinent questions about what socially conscious writing can hope to achieve today. The most immedi-

---

* An adaptation directed by David Cronenberg was released in 2012.

ately interesting parts have to do with the knots *Cosmopolis* ties itself into around the ideas of anti-capitalism and countercultural art in an age where "there's only one thing in the world worth pursuing professionally and intellectually ... the interaction between technology and capital." But beneath that puzzle lie some much more unsettling problems regarding what it is possible for us to think or imagine from within a society that seems almost superhumanly cruel.

The story depicts the last day in the life of Eric Packer, a 28-year-old asset-management billionaire living in New York in 2000. The plot is simple: in the morning, on a whim, Packer decides to take an eleven-block journey across Manhattan in his limo to get his hair cut at his favorite barbershop. En route he is waylaid by a series of symbolically loaded events, the most important of which is an enormous anti-capitalist riot in the middle of Times Square. After experiencing an epiphany at the sight of a protester setting himself on fire, Packer steadily loses or disposes of his assets. First he bankrupts himself; later he deliberately squanders his wife's fortune, murders his own bodyguard and abandons his car, before finally being assassinated by a disaffected ex-employee named Richard Sheets. The atmosphere in which all of this takes place is heavy with harbingers of catastrophe. The day the young billionaire crosses town is also the occasion for a spate of violent anarchist attacks. Banks are subjected to coordinated bombings, the head of the International Monetary Fund is murdered live on the Money Channel, and revolutionary slogans are projected onto the feed of the Stock Exchange (A SPECTER IS HAUNTING THE WORLD—THE SPECTER OF CAPITALISM). New York itself, where the best apartments command nine-figure sums and long white limousines have become "the most unnoticed vehicles" on the streets, is cast in one of the archetypal roles of apocalypse mythology: the decadent city on the brink of an abyss.

DeLillo remarked in a 2003 interview with the *Chicago Sun-Times* that *Cosmopolis* is "set on the last day of an era ... that interval between the end of the Cold War and the beginning of our current period of terror. It's essentially the 1990s." The manuscript was nearly finished when the 9/11 attacks took place, which meant that by the time the novel was published its moment had apparently already gone. All the signifiers the narrative is built around—the delirious market optimism of the Nineties, the digital boom, the newly unbridled capitalist expansionism and the mass protests against the G8 and the World Trade Organization—were supplanted in the general imagination by the twin specters of radical Islam and the War on Terror. But *Cosmopolis* had an uncanny afterlife. The story's date—April 2000—is significant not only for its millenarian overtones but also because that was the year the Dow Jones Industrial Average hit its (then) all-time peak, after which it fell into a two-year slump. The main action in the background to Packer's journey through New York is a massively leveraged bet he's made against the Japanese yen, a gamble that ultimately sinks his own company along with the entire global economy as *Cosmopolis* ends. (Hence the none-too-subtle double meaning of Packer's "getting a haircut"—business slang for accepting a loss on an investment.) In other words, the crisis the novel foretold was financial rather than terroristic. When the real crash arrived late in 2007 DeLillo's little fable of apocalyptic banking disasters and speculative hubris suddenly felt a lot more insightful. The relic of the Nineties became an omen of the present.

The idea of temporal glitches and irregularities—of things behind, ahead or outside of time—recurs over and over again inside *Cosmopolis*, too. In one of the book's recurring motifs, Packer's hyper-attuned faculties seem to merge with the pristine technology that surrounds him, giving him disturbing glimpses of the future moments before it takes place. To the capitalist's eyes, New York exists in a state of perpetual decay. No sooner does his gaze rest on some piece of technology—handheld phones, guns, cash registers, even the dazzling skyscrapers of the city's post-industrial economy—than it seems to rot into obsolescence. Indeed, you can see epochs melting into one another in the structure of the story itself, which layers futuristic fantasies and pop-culture clichés over the bones of an ancient warning about idolatry and greed. Packer himself is an almost overwhelmingly symbolic figure: a cross between Steve Jobs and one of Ayn Rand's titan capitalists, an all-purpose emblem of misbegotten utopianism, Faustian hubris and Babylonian wealth. Perhaps most conspicuously, he is also one of the latest in a long line of New York finance villains, the most famous of which belong to those late-Eighties spectacles of white-collar scandal and excess—Gordon Gekko in *Wall Street*, Sherman McCoy in *The Bonfire of the Vanities*, Patrick Bateman in *American Psycho*. DeLillo's billionaire is their digitally enhanced spawn: a young, handsome super-genius who "mastered the steepest matters in half an afternoon" and owns the most expensive apartment in New York, buying high-end luxuries on impulse and regularly indulging his heroic appetite for sex. (In Cronenberg's adaptation, the role is played by Robert Pattinson, an actor who owes his fame to the *Twilight* vampire films—a choice that neatly emphasizes the character's otherworldly glamour and evokes one of the oldest anti-capitalist vilifications there is: the bloodsucking parasite that takes society's product for its own.)

Gothic metaphors for capital go back as far as Marx, and the idea of money as an agent of pollution and moral sickness is older still. (In fact, this is another interesting component of Packer's character: the ancestral connection between finance capitalists and premodern usurers, men who were literally accused of

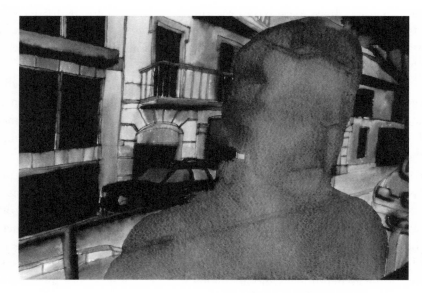

Danilo Santinelli, *Self-portrait*, 2012

stealing from God.*) Corruption—and the fear of corruption—runs all the way through *Cosmopolis*, along with an unshakeable current of despondency and frustration. In a 2005 interview with the French magazine *Panic*, DeLillo outlined part of the problem:

> You know, in America and in Western Europe we live in very wealthy democracies, we can do virtually anything we want, I'm able to write whatever I want to write. But I can't be part of this culture of simulation, in the sense of the culture's absorbing of everything. In doing that it neutralizes anything dangerous, anything that might threaten the consumer society. In *Cosmopolis* [a character] says, "What a culture does is absorb and neutralize its adversaries." If you're a writer who, one way or another, comes to be seen as dangerous, you'll wake up one morning and discover your face on a coffee mug or a t-shirt and you'll have been neutralized.

What's unsettling about the phenomenon DeLillo describes is that it doesn't seem to depend on anybody's intentions. It's just how consumer culture works: an impersonal mechanism with an apparently limitless capacity to assimilate dissent, as though every effort to evade the system's logic were somehow always and already enclosed within it. From his limo, Packer watches as anti-capitalist rioters attack banks and fight with the police in the heart of New York—another of the book's prophetic details, this time of the Occupy protests—but still he thought "there was a shadow of a transaction between the demonstrators and the state. The protest was a form of systematic hygiene ... It attested again, for the ten thousandth time, to the market culture's innovative brilliance, its ability to shape itself to its own flexible ends, absorbing everything around it." You don't need a sharp eye to pick up on the autoreferential subtext here: the demonstration that Packer regards as so ineffectual is already "contained" within the novel *Cosmopolis*, a marketized commodity. (One character goes so far as to call the riot a "market fantasy," which it literally is.)

For decades a certain kind of left-wing cultural theory has been formulating and reformulating the same impasse. Is it possible to mount any meaningful resistance to capitalism on the level of culture? Certainly in the West, after the Cold War, it has become extraordinarily difficult to believe that any amount of satire or critique could add up to systemic change. Quite the opposite: we've

---

* Jacques Le Goff's superb little book *La Bourse et la Vie* (1986) has a good account of this. Essentially, the usurer's crime was that he made money from the passage of time, but time belongs only to the Lord. There is a truly enormous amount of history tied up with the question of how such a cardinal sin eventually became the animating logic of our entire economy.

learned there's no such thing as a work of art or philosophy that's too dangerous to commodify. Packer's observations about the protest in Times Square come during a break in a lengthy conversation between himself and his "chief of theory" Vija Kinski, a corporate oracle who spouts slick aphorisms about the nature of time and money while people die and buildings burn around her (a grim caricature, perhaps, of the fate of radical theory after the end of history). The subject of their conversation is whether capitalism has a limit or not. It is Kinski who says that the market is total. The protest is a symptom of the destruction capitalism leaves in its wake, an anger that can only express itself in shapes that the market has already classified and absorbed years before. The demonstrators are "quotations," the burning man is a "quotation": nothing they do can threaten the basic conditions of their habitat. "There is nowhere they can go to be on the outside. There is no outside." Meanwhile, Packer watches as the anarchists flail uselessly around his car, as untouched as the system he represents.

F OR A LONG time the received wisdom about DeLillo was that he was a writer obsessed with paranoia (the critic Robert Towers once described him, wonderfully, as the "chief shaman of the paranoid school of American fiction") and certainly there's a great deal of post-Nixon fear and contempt for authority in his earlier work. But the truth is that paranoia and conspiracy theories were only ever components of a much larger concern with all of the unstable and self-defeating ways in which people try to divine order from the world. "The important thing about the paranoia in my characters is that it operates as a form of religious awe," DeLillo observed in his interview with the *Paris Review*. "It's something old, a leftover from some forgotten part of the soul." A similar thing could be said about any one of the conspicuous displays of learning in his novels. There's no shortage of academic catnip to do with philosophy, mathematics, consumerism, media theory, pop-culture iconography and so on. But the cleverness is almost always a channel for something more primal—dread and fascination, the sense of a structure above or below our capacities to articulate it. His writing can be off-putting in the way that less successful conceptual art can be—marked by a "fastidious vagueness," as James Wood has put it. Yet at its best it emits an insistent, sub-rational tremor: dreamlike in the particular sense that it seems to cry out for an interpretation even if there's no way of telling what the "real" message is or could be.

On the surface, it's not easy to understand how this subliminal technique fits with DeLillo's forcefully political ideas about what literature is for. "Writers must oppose systems," he told *Panic*. "It's important to write against power, corporations, the state, and the whole system of consumption and of debilitating entertainments. ... Writers, by nature, must oppose things, oppose whatever power tries to impose on us." The answer to this puzzle lies in the type of power that interests DeLillo. Politics, in his hands, is presented as a struggle for imaginative control, one in which it doesn't take much to fall victim to malign forces. His books return over and over to figures who have the ability to shape or command the thoughts of others: fanatics, demagogues, cultists, advertisers, celebrities, crooks—and artists. In a famous scene from *Mao II* (1991), DeLillo's novelist-hero speculates that writers and terrorists are engaged in a zero-sum struggle. "What terrorists gain, novelists lose. The degree to which they influence mass consciousness is the extent of our decline as shapers of sensibility and thought. The danger they represent equals our own failure to be dangerous."*

Cosmopolis revisits the idea of a clandestine war for the world's imagination, although in this case the novelist's counterpart is a businessman rather than a terrorist. Packer is a human forecasting instrument, reading the future and shaping the lives of untold billions from his car in the middle of Manhattan. "You know things. I think this is what you do," says his wife over breakfast. "I think you're dedicated to knowing. I think you acquire information and turn it into something stupendous and awful. You're a dangerous person. Do you agree? A visionary." Like his *Wall Street*-era predecessors, Packer belongs to an economy in which information about commodities is more valuable than the commodities themselves. The difference is that the market he represents has ascended to an unprecedented level of speed, scope and abstraction. At the beginning of his career he made his fortune forecasting stocks, but before long "history became monotonous and slobbering, yielding to his search for something purer, for techniques of charting that predicted the movements of money itself." Abstract knowledge is what underlies Packer's status. And information is his object of worship—the testament to a clean and secret harmony behind the manifest world:

---

* DeLillo expands on this thought elsewhere, describing Beckett and Kafka as writers whose "inner world ... eventually folded into the three-dimensional world we were all living in." For all of his talk about novelists as the opponents of oppressive systems of manipulation, what's striking about this image of successful writing is how conspiratorial it is, if not also a little creepy. The author, alone in a room, exerts his secret power over how the world sees and thinks—a kind of hidden overlord or controller.

Danilo Santinelli, *Vincenzo*, 2012

He looked ... towards streams of numbers running in opposite directions. He understood how much it meant to him, the roll and flip of data on a screen. He studied the figural diagrams that brought organic patterns into play, birdwing and chambered shell. It was shallow thinking to maintain that numbers and charts were the cold compression of unruly human energies, every sort of yearning and midnight sweat reduced to lucid units in the financial markets. In fact data itself was soulful and glowing, a dynamic aspect of the life process. This was the eloquence of alphabets and numeric systems, now fully realized in electronic form, in the zero-oneness of the world, the digital imperative that defined every breath of the planet's living billions. Here was the heave of the biosphere. Our bodies and oceans were here, knowable and whole.

Packer's data is a living map of Earth: a vision of the world as a single huge organism held together by money and technology, a manmade fact so enormous it can only be represented as a cross between abstraction and mystic epiphany. In the capitalist's exaltations, the logic of accumulation and the religious sublime dissolve into one, a fantasy of ultimate triumph over ignorance and uncertainty, and hence risk—insider information at its most cosmic. What's a terrorist's strength compared to all this?

What, indeed, is a writer's? The palpable thrill that DeLillo gives off as he describes Packer's unearthly powers is in stark contrast to the dull familiarity of *Cosmopolis*'s anti-capitalist tropes. In a sense that's exactly the point: the capitalist's way of thinking is so formidable it is hard to imagine any genuine opposition to it. Violence has always stalked DeLillo's work, and—as critics have pointed out—it's often implicitly presented as the only viable response to the sickness of modern society. But in *Cosmopolis* neither theory nor force seems like an answer to the great webs of encircling power DeLillo evokes. Even if the demonstrators were incited to kill him, thinks Packer, what difference would it make to the system? Although DeLillo spends plenty of time worrying about being complicit with the market, the deeper quandary isn't about money or selling out. Rather, it's a replay of another one of the fundamental problems of countercultural thought: How can the product of a society—be it a person or a piece of art—be *against* that society? Where does the critical distance come from? The point isn't that these questions are new, but that it has become harder and harder to know how to answer them in a world where capitalism appears as an almost fully naturalized fact of existence, and where there may not be space for an alternative even inside our heads.

ELEVEN YEARS AFTER it was published, *Cosmopolis*'s barely suppressed sense of fatalism doesn't seem unjustified. The crash it presaged happened, but the system carried on as if no thinkable alternative existed—and in a way DeLillo's novel seems to have foreseen that, too. After he witnesses a protester immolating himself only yards from his limousine, Packer begins to go mad. Night falls. He leaves his car and continues on foot through the streets of New York until a dreamy coincidence puts him into the path of Richard Sheets, a former currency analyst in his company who has been plotting against him for months or maybe years. The two men have a lengthy back and forth about why Sheets wants to murder Packer, then the capitalist allows himself to be killed. By the time of his death most of Packer's vampiric charisma is long gone, and the pulse of the story has vanished. In fact, the most interesting thing about *Cosmopolis*'s final scene is the return of that faint but distinct edge of self-criticism. Sheets, although at first he presents himself as a warrior for social justice, is quickly unmasked as a blubbering psychopath. Packer waves him away as a "cheap imitation" and a "stale fantasy." Indeed the ending might seem to confirm the judgment of the novel's critics. Is *Cosmopolis* just another lump of useless, pseudo-radical critique?

But it's idle to describe something as a failure if we don't have any meaningful idea of what success looks like. Part of the trouble with anti-capitalist art in general is that it is vague—it almost never seems to know what it's asking for or even exactly what its object of attack is. "Capitalism" itself is a term that expands or contracts depending on who is using it, a signifier for a whole range of very different and not obviously compatible things, viz. a more or less narrow structure of economic organization, an impersonal global process, an ideology, a culture, modernity, the Western world, big business, a way of behaving and thinking that penetrates the most intimate aspects of everyday life and so on. In order to fight the evils of the system, you would have to know where the system ends. But where does it end? Without an answer it's not clear what "real" political art would be—at least as far as capitalism and anti-capitalism are concerned—let alone how to make it effective.

From a certain angle, DeLillo's story might look like a cynical parody of protest art, or else some oblique argument to the effect that authentic anti-capitalism is impossible. But I don't think either of those ideas quite captures it. It would be better to say that *Cosmopolis* is using anti-capitalism to ask a question: What's it like to live in a society where we can't imagine any convincing alternative? DeLillo has said he doesn't think his books could have been written in the world that existed before the JFK assassination, and the reasons he gives are bound up with his idea that the event injected a fatal dose of incoherence into American life. In *The Word, the Image, and the Gun*, a documentary DeLillo made in 1991 with the BBC, he explained:

> When Kennedy was shot something changed forever in America, something opened up a sense of randomness, deep ambiguity, we lost the narrative thread. ... The assassination left an emptiness that left everything plausible, made us susceptible to the most incredible ideas and fantasies. We couldn't seem to find out what happened even on the most basic level: how many gunmen, how many shots, how many wounds on the President's body. There was no coherent reality we analyze and study. So we became a little paranoid. We developed a sense of the secret manipulation of history. You know: there's something they aren't telling us.

"An emptiness that left everything plausible." In *The Names* (1982), one character describes America as "the world's living myth"—by which he means that the USA is the organizing principle of modern history, the master narrative around which the rest of the world has to arrange itself. Yet the central irony of DeLillo's work is that this era of unprecedented hegemony coincided with a deep sense of plotlessness and disintegrity, a hole in the nation's heart that needed to be perpetually compensated for.

Cosmopolis, set just after the end of the American Century, is partially about the death of that old "living myth" way of thinking (or rather its subversion by new, supranational forces of commerce). But it's also another episode in DeLillo's long rumination on the secret or missing structure of American life, reformulated for an era when society's organizing code feels less like it's concealed within some government vault and more as if it's wired into the occult rhythms of commerce. Just before the riot engulfs Packer's car, Kinski makes a cryptic analogy between art and money. "Money has lost its narrative quality the way painting did once upon a time," she says. "Money is talking to itself." One way to understand the remark is as an oblique reference to modernism, the period where art first became "difficult," where its meaning and purpose—and so also its methods and effects—no longer seemed to make sense in the old way.* Insofar as the complexities of contemporary finance make it a challenge

---

* It was also, to extrapolate a little, the birth of the idea that artistic success could be morally or politically problematic—that in obeying institutionalized norms for what counts as "good art" you might inadvertently feed into a mendacious or oppressive social system. *Cosmopolis* doesn't make a huge fuss over the point, but the fact that Packer is shown contemplating a bid for the Rothko Chapel—so that he can install the whole thing into his luxury apartment—says plenty about how threatening the modernist project looks today, at least to rich people.

Danilo Santinelli, *Drive*, 1998

to figure out what has happened in the world market and how, money might be said to have become "difficult" too. Bleeding-edge capitalism, as somebody once remarked, resembles nothing so much as a new form of abstruse conceptual art, the rarefied dominion of an insular cosmopolitan elite whose activities appear—but only appear—to have no roots in the everyday world.

But however Kinski's remark is meant to be understood, one of its implications is clear: if money has no narrative quality, then a society built around moneymaking has no story either. That sounds enigmatic, but I take it that DeLillo is trying to say something about the idea of legitimacy. After all, what is it for a society to *have* a narrative? In the most basic sense, it means it has an explanation for itself, some shared account of what makes it the way it is. In which case, to say that a society lacks a narrative is a way of saying that it's senseless, that it can't be explained in terms of what's good for the people who populate it (the only real justification a social order can have). Even Packer is a victim. When we first meet him, the billionaire is roaming around his apartment before dawn, sleepless and upset about his inability to chart the yen. "There is an order at some deep level," he says to Kinski, explaining the problem. "A pattern that wants to be seen." But the riddle refuses to be solved, and Packer's crisis metastasizes until he's lost his grip on the world completely. ("Do you get the feeling sometimes," asks one of his associates early in the day, "that you don't know what's going on?"—the question recurs in various forms throughout the book.) There's plenty of evidence in *Cosmopolis* to suggest we're supposed to see Packer as a kind of artist in meltdown, someone whose desire for beauty and precision has been poisoned by doubts and self-disgust. He's consumed with uncertainty about his work, obsesses over the question of whether his creations are true to the world and despises the thought of being unoriginal. But he can't think of any effective way to proceed—a dilemma that aptly, if unfortunately, reflects that of the novel he belongs to.

"WE LEAD MORE interesting lives than we think," thinks one of the conspirators in *Libra*. "We are characters in plots, without the compression and numinous sheen. Our lives, examined carefully in all their affinities and links, abound with suggestive meaning, with themes and involute turnings we have not allowed ourselves to see completely." It is impossible to read DeLillo's work for long without picking up on the sense of yearning for a providential structure, as well as the awful feeling of separation from any such unifying plot. It's probably no accident that out of the whole range of emotions the one he describes most powerfully is grief ("chaos and divergences," as he once described it, "foes of God") or that he should be so enchanted by the idea of interpretation, since each represents a type of human response to disorder. The same inclination underlies much of what's playful in his work. Murray, the university professor who acts as a kind of built-in theorist and critic in *White Noise*, loves nothing better than to extol the endless lure of explanation and analysis:

> Everything is concealed in symbolism, hidden by veils of mystery and layers of cultural material. But it is psychic data, absolutely. ... It is just a question of deciphering, rearranging, peeling off the layers of unspeakability. Not that we would want to, not that any useful purpose would be served.

That last sentence is important—and it's this tantalizing and self-censuring quality that sometimes makes DeLillo's writing feel like a bleak joke at the expense of the type of person who is attracted to it, a lure that pulls you in but never takes you anywhere. *Cosmopolis* is exemplary in this respect. On the one hand, the sheer allegorical density of the book is extraordinary: the text is so full of teasing symbolism, suggestive patterns, cunning literary references and allusions to theory that once you start trying to add it all up it quickly becomes overwhelming.* Yet it fits with the generally demoralized tenor of the novel that what all of this incredible allusiveness seems to *convey* in the end is something closer to frustration or inarticulacy, an infectious unease that makes it difficult to be either satisfied by DeLillo's book or indifferent towards it.

The philosopher Georg Lukács once said that there was something nightmarish in the experience of an intellectual with no vision of the future. Underneath all of its obstructions and code, DeLillo's writing seems to express the

---

* To give just one example, the title—from the Greek *kosmopolis*, "world-city"—is conceivably a reference to Saskia Sassen's *The Global City* (1991), a pioneering study of the rising importance of major metropolitan hubs (such as New York) in the worldwide economy. It could also very easily be taken as a nod to Plato's *Republic*, the ur-text of Western political theory and the original instance of the city employed as a metaphor for psychic health. Put the two sources together and you get a nice line about how Packer's downfall might symbolize the compromised integrity of the prevailing world order and the inner discord it breeds in its citizens. And this is only to scratch the surface. Even if you were to filter out everything other than political philosophy, you could still find connections—overt or subliminal—made to the writings of Aristotle, Hegel, Adam Smith, Marx, Walter Benjamin, the Frankfurt School, Jacques Derrida, Jean Baudrillard, Gilles Deleuze, Félix Guattari, Guy Debord, Fredric Jameson, Michael Hardt, Antonio Negri, Francis Fukuyama, and no doubt many others. If you were so inclined you might also tease out the links that DeLillo seems to set up between abstract art and suicide, or explore Packer's repressed homoeroticism, or the numerous references to the Icarus myth and the allegedly poisonous nature of technocratic utopianism; the list goes on. *Cosmopolis* seems to secrete meanings at a rate that outstrips the mind's capacity to organize them.

same thought. The future is a kind of narrative category, after all: the projected goal that gives the present its sense of order and purpose. It's something we suffer without. For an individual, the inability to imagine life improving, or changing in any way other than badly, is a kind of death sentence. On the collective level, too, a society without any aspirations toward a better shared existence is condemned to the unchallenged perpetuation of injustice and misery, the ineradicable underside of all human history to date (and a horror that weighs "like a nightmare" on the living, as Marx so famously put it). DeLillo's entire project has been based on a sense of disorientation that's fundamentally political—the loss of a collective narrative, the transformation of a once-shared experience of America into something enigmatic and foreign. Part of Lukács's point was that a society can't suffer something like that without the damage making itself felt in everyday life, through all the sensations that DeLillo has spent his career so expertly evoking: confusion, anomie, anxiety, isolation, fear.

The obvious question is then: What would it be to overcome that? The most electrifying moments in *Cosmopolis* are gestures in the direction of an immense world order beyond the limits of ordinary perception. Packer's enchanted map of Earth is one; another arrives as he and Kinski stare up at a massive electronic display of market information, "three tiers of data running concurrently and swiftly about a hundred feet above the street," a glittering maze "of numbers and symbols, the fractions, decimals, stylized dollar signs, the streaming release of words ... [not a] flow of information so much as pure spectacle, or information made sacred, ritually unreadable." The imagery is marvelous and alienating, a premonition of a vast globalized unity that we are all now part of, but one that seems to be hopelessly hidden from sight—and a repository for all of the book's stillborn political dreams. "I understand none of it," is the mantra Kinski repeats whenever she is brought face to face with the miracles of capitalist technology, and the point is perhaps that it's laughable to imagine that our minds could ever acquire purchase on something as supernaturally complex as our own society. There are moments in the book where we catch sight of the less fortunate world beyond the borders of New York, places where the free market has visited little except destruction and chaos. But it seems telling that these images never advance beyond the edges of the plot. They belong to our story and they don't—symbols for the parts of the system we can't countenance or even fully register.

Yet it would be wrong to say that everything feels finished once *Cosmopolis* ends. Despite its resolutely grim conclusion, some spectral sense of possibility remains—the feeling that perhaps, even so, all of this has just been the prelude for something larger and new. Whatever else, the novel is a testament to the strength of DeLillo's vision: the world he has been imagining for so long really does seem to have folded out into reality. Dissolving national identities, missing narratives, complicity, powerlessness—aren't they just facts of globalized life? The intimation that we are all part of a single huge, unseen story has also come closer and closer to lived experience, and our most urgent collective problems (the looming ecological catastrophe, for example) reflect it. But it still feels like more than we can imagine. What would it be to tell such a story—to assimilate its mind-breaking scale, the networks of superhuman technology and the anonymous billions who populate it? For whom could it be anything more than an abstraction? *Cosmopolis* falls apart before it comes close to answering those questions. But the questions are real. The world demands a response. The riddle is how to become the type of creatures that can give it.

Kate MacDowell, *Mice and Men*, 2009
All photographs taken by Dan Kvitka

THE TRAGIC DIET

FOOD AND FINITUDE

by S. G. Belknap

LIVING IN THE kinds of apartments I do means mice, often. House mice, one of the world's most successful species—whatever that means—don't care how much money we pay for our apartments in Park Slope, in Back Bay, in Bay Heights, Bay Slope, Slope Heights. They love the tenderness of the wood floors beneath our 1920s radiators; they love the dusty corridors behind our bookshelves. Even if they are not inside our rooms, they are in our basements or walls, in most of our buildings, most of the time.

There is an art to removing mice from an apartment. Cats are not as effective as folk wisdom would have us believe: some cats are good "mousers"; most are not. The typical urbanite response of "putting out a few traps" to "catch the mouse" is woefully inadequate, not least because no one ever has *a* mouse— mice are social animals like humans or dogs, not loners like cats of prey. We also seem to be inadvertently breeding trap-resistant strains of mice: these little acrobats are the stars of internet videos, tip-toeing their way into peanut butter as night-vision cameras look on. Stopping up holes doesn't always work, because it is an invitation for new holes; mice are artists of direction, intimately familiar with the geography of walls and cabinets—indeed, this is why they and their rat cousins love mazes so much. The best solution appears to be the one-two punch of an aggressive, almost exorbitant, trapping regimen followed by the plugging up of entrances. You must kill all the mice who have "knowledge" about your apartment; you must wipe out an entire mouse culture.

Before I knew this I made the mistake of setting out a single sticky trap in my living room as a kind of mouse detector. My girlfriend and I had spotted a scout rounding the corner one evening as we watched *Lost*. That night the gaps between the floor and floorboards that were not already filled with steel wool got some steel wool of their own. In a few days we started to sleep better, but just to be sure we set out that single sticky trap along the wall. Two weeks went by before I heard my girlfriend's gasp from the front room.

The mouse was sprawled out on its abdomen, all four limbs pointing away from its body as if pulled there by ropes. At first I wasn't sure that it was even alive: with its entire lower half glued to the plastic, including the bottom of its head, there was nowhere to move—would I even be able to tell if it was breathing? Do mice close their eyes when they die? As I got closer and closer, hovering over it, it moved, trying again what it had surely tried hundreds of times already: it jerked its body from back to front, propelling itself and the plate of plastic forward and backward, like a canoe without an oar.

Having a captive living mouse in your apartment is a bit like seeing a sick raccoon limping down the street during the day, or a giant squid tossed up on a beach: a creature that thrives on darkness is suddenly there at your disposal, available for pushing or prodding or experimentation. You could talk to it, you could tell it jokes; you could set it down on the couch to watch TV with you. We did none of those things, but we never forgot that we could have, even as we went hunting for the tools of extermination.

We had a large mallet made of hard rubber, which I figured would be perfect for the job. But I couldn't simply deliver a blow in the open: the force of it would send blood everywhere. So I picked up the mouse and its boat with a pair of rubber gloves and put them inside a plastic grocery bag. But surely one bag was not enough—it would tear, right? I wrapped another one around.

I stepped out into the stairwell, looking for a harder striking surface. The linoleum there was fine, but I could hear the neighbors rustling next door, so I thought it better to go outside. On the way downstairs I passed another resident of the building, who didn't seem to notice, or care, that I was wearing yellow rubber gloves and carrying a mallet and a plastic bag. Out on the New York City street I waited pointlessly for a gap in foot traffic, the bag next to me on the stoop, the mouse thinking who knows what. I decided to go back upstairs. Ten minutes had passed.

Only when it finally came time to bring the mallet down—on the linoleum after all, not that it matters—did it occur to me that I had no way of knowing if I would be able to hit cleanly. I couldn't see through two plastic bags, and that left only one option, an option I could not bring myself to choose, or even think about for very long: to lay my hand on his body, to wrap my hand around him, like holding a nail in place to drive it home. He would wiggle, right? He would protest somehow, and I would feel the bones of his back through his skin. He would, in some way or other, respond to my touch. I couldn't do it, and so he and I didn't do it, and we just got on with the thing.

The first blow must have missed his brain, because I heard a squeak. It was oddly cut off, as if his lungs or larynx had suddenly filled with blood. Maybe if I had been closer to him I would have heard a little mouse gurgle, or some miniscule sputtering. I hammered again, about seven more times, covering a circle around where I had hit before. There was no more noise—but what did that mean? I was sure I had to open the bags and look, but I was also sure that the injured mouse, his limbs somehow unstuck by the pounding, would limp out onto my hands and then the floor, dragging blood with him, contaminating me and accusing me with his eyes. I unwrapped the first plastic bag. The inner bag had torn and blood had leaked through into the outer. I unwrapped the inner bag and found him, or at least found something. It was a mass of fur and flesh, a jumble of vaguely organic material, the kind of thing you occasionally see nature do on her own, like when a cat gives birth to a foot with some teeth attached. I guess you could say the hammering had been successful, then—there was nothing more to do with that mouse. What was left went into the trash downstairs, and the rubber gloves went with it.

I

A FEW YEARS AGO I stopped being a vegetarian, started eating a lot of meat, and lost about fifteen pounds. I had heard about paleo dieting from my brother, and it was good to me: that late-twenties pudge on my stomach and lower back more or less melted away; my skin got clearer; I no longer needed to take a nap every afternoon after lunch. I enjoyed looking in the mirror again. And all I had to do—to make a long story short—was to take the bread out of my diet and replace it with meat.

Yes, I was an ethical vegetarian. But when I first took the leap, drawn in by the promise of weight loss, I was somehow able to put my reservations on hold. Within a few weeks they seemed to disappear entirely. Spreading butter on top of my beef, or wiping the animal fat off the sides of my kitchen sink, I was charmed. It was as if my body had hijacked my mind: I stopped internally citing Genesis 1:29—God only gave us plants and fruits to eat—and started up with Cain and Abel instead—God accepts the little lambs of the shepherd Abel, and not the fruits of the farmer Cain. And after years and years of my own vegetarianism, I caught myself sneering at vegetarians, annoyed whenever I had to accommodate them. I was a man obsessed. The thing about obsession, however, is that it tends to wear off. As time went by, the old concerns found their way into my consciousness bit by bit. And then one day I destroyed a mouse with a hammer.

VEGETARIANISM HAS BEEN the official diet of polite society for some decades now. Even those who eat meat acknowledge indirectly in one way or other that it is unhealthy. Some indulge occasionally and carefully, figuring that if they keep the frequency down they won't die young, and won't be denying themselves one of life's little pleasures. Some stick to the relatively benign choices, like salmon and chicken breast—meat that is light on the plate and light in the belly. All, however, assume that no meat, or very little, would be best, and all assume that the ideal diet looks like what Whole Foods tells us it looks like: quinoa and olive oil, walnuts and blueberries, and a lot of what is green and bright and scratchy. No one in the last forty years has thought that eating a steak every day was a healthful, or even non-insane, course of action. No one until now, that is. This is the scandal of paleo: that someone—and not just anyone, because it is your friend, or your relative or your co-worker—is making the case that eating a steak every day is a perfectly normal thing to do. And not just a perfectly normal thing to do, but the best thing to do, and, by the way, what *you* should do. If you are not already a paleo eater, then you have had your ear talked off by one. That friend or relative or coworker has trapped you in an elevator or a moving car, and has preached to you. You were told to change your ways; you were warned of your corporeal damnation. And it was awkward. If we were once unified in our ideas about health, we are not anymore. There is a schism within the class of readers and chatterers.

As with all schisms, the internet is to blame. The modern paleo movement did begin before the digital age: there was Boyd Eaton's 1985 article in the *New England Journal of Medicine*, "Paleolithic nutrition: A consideration of its nature and current implications"; and there were a few books and studies here and there by authors who have now become folk heroes of paleo, like Staffan Lindeberg and Loren Cordain. But the first decade of the new century brought the full force of the internet, and with it a proliferation of paleo theorizing. The ideas of the movement—along with recipes and a whole lot of idle talk—found their way into homes and offices, and before long some of the people in those homes and offices started buying what the internet was selling.

The majority of paleo conversions probably begin with the website Mark's Daily Apple. Its curator, Mark Sisson, defies nature and common sense in possessing an ultra-sculpted upper torso at over 60 years old, a torso so persuasive it is plastered on every corner of the site. Those wishing to attain his physique—and some do succeed, judging by the before-and-after pictures—can put into their bodies what Sisson does: a lot of vegetables, a lot of meat, a lot of fats that we used to think were forbidden (butter and beef tallow *don't* cause heart disease!), and some potatoes here and there. If we are to believe him, Sisson every day prepares what he calls his "big-ass salad," the fresh ingredients for which he has stowed in a special refrigerator compartment built into the kitchen counter of his improbably sunlit Southern California home. Dinner is a big slab of beef or bison and some cooked vegetables, with red wine and dark chocolate as occasional indulgences. (Some meat is saved for the following day's big-ass salad.)

Sisson's image is not the only one gracing the website. Mark's Daily Apple has a pre-agricultural mascot named "Grok," who may wear an animal skin and wield a spear, but who appears—we only have a silhouette—to have the normal, full-sized forehead of *Homo sapiens*. Grok is the condensation of the evolutionary theorizing that underlies most of Sisson's recommendations: we should avoid soybean oil and corn oil because pre-agricultural man, a.k.a. Grok, did not have access to them; we should occasionally sprint and "lift heavy things" because pre-agricultural man, a.k.a. Grok, did; and so on, for sleep (remove artificial light from your bedroom, because Grok slept in the dark), sunlight (you need it for vitamin D, and Grok never sat in an office), and stress (keep it short and intense, like running from a lion; Grok never worried about a promotion). Partisans of the website encourage each other to "Grok on," and often indulge in "Grokfests" back home, which can involve boulder-carrying contests, loincloths and piles of barbecued meat.

Inspiring as the caveman motif has been to many, to others in the paleo world it has been positively irritating. Women, perhaps not surprisingly, are not always comfortable with a narrative that seems to have only two places for them: gathering berries or being pulled by their hair into a cave. About three years ago the paleo movement began a self-criticism from a scientific angle as well, which has led to a widespread de-Grokification (although, to be fair, Mark Sisson himself has been mostly on board). The gist of the revision is this: we should not eat like cavemen because, as it turns out, we are not cavemen. Human beings were not done evolving 10,000 years ago, when agriculture and animal husbandry began to take over the Western world. We are different now: a great many of us human beings, for example, have found a way to keep our small intestines full of lactase—the enzyme that lets us drink milk—well into adulthood. And the bacteria that live in our guts (by some estimates a population ten times greater than "our own" cells) have spent thousands of years happily evolving, adapting to the food we eat. The theoretical shift has been profound enough to be marked by a new name: the movement is now the "ancestral health movement," the diet an "ancestral diet." And meat? It has fallen from its pedestal. Bloggers can now admit that they eat something other than raw ground beef: potatoes, say, or buckwheat pancakes, or legumes, or even dessert (provided it is made with lard or cream, of course). The ancestral world is a kinder, gentler place.

If there is a figure emerging as the guide for the new movement, it is Paul Jaminet. Jaminet (feel free to Frenchify that last syllable) is a former Harvard astrophysicist who, along with his molecular biologist wife Shou-Ching, published the cheerily titled *Perfect Health Diet* in 2010. Faced with chronically *non*-perfect health, Jaminet decided to spend five years researching biochemistry and nutrition to do something about it, and succeeded. The PHD—so the diet is usually called—bears the impress of Jaminet's quiet, synthesizing intellect: the diet feels *complete* in a way that earlier paleo diets did not. Gone is the weirdly particular big-ass salad; gone is the weirdly austere ribeye à la carte. A PHD dinner has it all. There is a portion of meat, usually a pastured ruminant (beef, lamb, bison), gently cooked, about half a pound. There is a modest portion of starch (potato, sweet potato, taro, even rice—the most innocuous of the grains), but always mixed with fat, because starch and fat complement each other nicely in the process of digestion. There is an acid somewhere, like vinegar or lemon juice, perhaps in a sauce; acids help the body break down fat. There are vegetables: fresh ones and cooked ones. And there are fermented vegetables too, because the bacteria in the gut need replenishing. And there is bone stock, consumed as soup, or mixed into the starch. All of the elements work together: a perfect whole.

The real importance of Jaminet's work, however, might not be a matter of synthesis, but of emphasis. Just as much as any other ancestral nutritionist, Jaminet reminds us what we *shouldn't* eat: grains, vegetable oils, sugar—what the blogger Kurt Harris called the "neolithic agents of disease." But in addition he spends more time telling us what we *should* eat. Jaminet has convinced the ancestral health movement of the importance of adequate "micronutrition": making sure we get the whole alphabet soup of vitamins and minerals into our bodies on a regular basis. One way to do this, certainly, is by taking pills—and Jaminet does recommend supplements as a kind of insurance policy. A better way to do it is by eating foods that are rich in nutrients. From the ancestral perspective, the federal government's well-meaning advice to eat heaps of vegetables every day is insufficient, or possibly even detrimental; vegetables do not really pack the nutritional punch we think they do, in large part because their micronutrients are not easily assimilated by our bodies. The *real* goods are a group of foods that Jaminet calls "supplemental foods," and almost all of them come from an animal: egg yolks, liver, kidney, oysters, fish eggs, soups made from bones and joints. Vegetables have their place in a "perfect" diet, sure, but the supplemental foods are the aristocrats of the entire food kingdom. We will need to eat them if we want to be, in one of the ancestral world's beloved phrases, *well nourished.*

The shift from paleo to ancestral saw meat fall, then, but it dusted itself off and is here to stay. In the eyes of the ancestral movement, animals just are the special place where nature's bounty gathers and condenses; the animals have sifted through the world of plants (or smaller animals) and collected for us what is best, storing it up in their organs and bones and embryos. The thought is not without anthropological precedent. The recent reorientation has focused attention on an author who spent years studying the diets of isolated peoples, back when isolated peoples still existed: Weston A. Price. Price is the closest thing the ancestral movement has to a classic thinker, and his 1939 book *Nutrition and Physical Degeneration* the closest thing the movement has to a classic text. The book is a compendium of Price's travels to little-known and little-visited parts of the world, where he and his wife managed to secure samples of food and saliva, and photographs of teeth, from all manner of "natives." What Price found—in the Canadian and Alaskan subarctic, in the forests of central Africa, in the remote archipelagos of the South Pacific—was nothing short of miraculous, by our standards at least: the "primitives" were in a condition of splendid health. In every corner of the globe Price uncovered tribe after tribe untouched by heart disease, cancer and diabetes, all with resilient bodies, all with beautiful, smiling faces. For Price this had everything to do with food—and with certain special foods in particular. Every one of Price's native cultures had its own set of "supplemental foods" just like Jaminet's: foods they went to great lengths to attain; parts and products of animals that went first to expectant mothers, children and the old, but went to everyone eventually and were universally valued. For the tundra-dwelling Native Americans it was the organs of moose and other large animals. For the Alpine Swiss it was milk (although they ate their fair share of flesh as well). For Melanesian and Polynesian islanders it was shellfish—and here Price has a rather remarkable story to tell. Inland-dwelling groups on larger islands, accustomed to trade with the islanders along the shore for the precious shellfish, sometimes had to resort to cannibalism. When they did, they targeted fishermen, whose livers had built up more of the desired nutrients.

We in the modern West assume that the conquest of nature by the medical sciences has guaranteed us a level of health previously unseen on the planet—if South Sea islanders were eating each other, well then, that was only to avoid starving. But in Price's mind, the radiant health of his isolated peoples tells a different story. We are the ones in poor health. We are the ones with malnutrition. And Price went even further: We are the ones who are "degenerating." We are passing down our nutritional deficiencies from generation to generation, and with every generation the effect is worse. We pour millions and millions of dollars into researching the diseases we get—but if we had eaten differently, and our parents had eaten differently, and our grandparents had eaten differently, then we wouldn't be getting those diseases in the first place. Price's dramatic conclusion is accepted by many ancestral eaters today, who routinely bemoan their own epigenetic inheritance, or assume that a vegan is simply coasting on the hardy constitution handed down to him by his parents. If the ancestrals are right, then meat plays a much bigger role in human nutrition than we have been led to believe. We may not need a steak every day—but we cannot flourish, it seems, without animals.

I AM NOT SURE how much of this I accept, ultimately. At the moment I do find a lot of it convincing, and what I have read about paleo and ancestral is in large part responsible for my eating the way I do. But I have been a devoted partisan of so many diets in the past—vegetarianism, veganism, and even, for one year, a no-mammal policy—that I hesitate to shout this newest one from the rooftops. My mother asks me before every holiday what I am eating; it always seems so self-evident to me, at least until the next time I get this unflattering reminder of my wishy-washiness. And despite my general agreement with the ancestral template I've found that attempts to "do my homework," to be "absolutely sure" about the best human diet, are essentially useless: studies in modern journals try their best to squeeze nutrition into a box, but it just keeps bursting out from the other side. There are simply too many factors to tame; and scientists, despite their best intentions, build their own biases into their experiments, confirming the superiority of their favorite diet in ever-changing ways. Nowadays I let my eyes glaze over when I read the inevitable declaration of confidence from an author writing on nutrition, whether it is the vegan T. Colin Campbell, the "flexitarian" Michael Pollan or one of my own ancestrals. "After years of study I have determined that..."—Let me stop you right there, as they say.

But despite all of my inconstancy and all of my skepticism—and all the hours lost to learning biochemistry—there is something that I am fairly sure of now, and it seems unlikely to change: I thrive on the flesh and milk of animals. I'd like to be able to say that I knew this from the first time I ate meat after my long hiatus: a grass-fed steak from an upscale steakhouse in Chicago, the lofty price somehow justified by the details of my steer's pedigree on the back of the menu. My body may have been in shock that day—but it didn't last long. In the following weeks eating meat became a contemplative, even epiphanous, experience. I would take a bite of my steak and then sit still with my hands together in my lap, head turned down, eyes closed and mouth chewing. I imagined I could feel the nutrients warming my heart, and then coursing through my arteries to my extremities. If other people were around it was a little embarrassing. The whole thing felt like falling in love, or finding the film or the novel that stops everything in your life from spinning. Something or other just felt *right*. It felt like I and the world were made for each other; there was something in the world that was designed for me, and I was finally getting it.

I eat less meat than I used to. At my peak my diet consisted of little else than a daily dose of two pounds of beef. Before long I was down to about a pound, and then half a pound—and sometimes just a quarter of a pound. I took a hint from the downward trend and tried eliminating meat altogether. It didn't work. In my experiments I found that if I don't get a minimal amount of meat, or at the very least some chicken stock or beef stock, then I suffer. I feel the same uncomfortable deprivation I felt as a vegetarian, passing by my neighbor's door while she had a roast in the oven: not just a desire, but something deeper than that. A demand, maybe.

II

BACK IN MY student days I saw a philosophy professor change his mind about dogs. He had claimed in a lecture that dogs are essentially machines, programmed to make themselves appealing to authorities, and I was rankled in the way you can only be rankled when someone you look up to disagrees with you about something big. Two years later he got a family dog and by all appearances loved her very much. When I ran into him in the park with my own dog, he felt qualified to give me advice on a number of topics, like brands of kibble and the canine need for companionship; he may have even used the word "play-dates." It doesn't take much time for love to make you an expert, apparently.

I have been an animal person for as long as I can remember, and that is long enough to have learned that there is no use in trying to persuade someone

Kate MacDowell, *Romulus and Remus*, 2009

who isn't an animal person to become one. You may as well try to persuade someone to become a Republican or a Democrat or to prefer brunettes; persuasion just doesn't seem to be a relevant kind of activity in these cases. It takes experience to change: real experience, lived experience. My philosophy professor's transformation from cold-eyed cynic to glowing animal person came about not because he had dedicated more thought to the issue, but because, to put it simply, he had lived with an animal for a while. He *felt* his way into the new perspective; he didn't *reason* his way into it. I imagine his philosopher's pride took a hit in the process.

But reason still dominates in academic philosophy, and academic philosophy, directly or indirectly, dominates our discourse about animals. From the philosopher's perspective, the human mind is the measure of all living beings. Whether we should eat animals or not depends on whether or not they live up to our cognitive standards. Do animals possess an authentic self-awareness? Can they use language? If they can, is it only mimicry? Can they use language to refer to itself? Can they press a lever to give a fellow animal a treat? The hoops we ask animals to jump through are always chosen by us, and they always flatter us. The "mirror test," for example—which chimpanzees pass with flying colors, bless them—challenges its subject to remove an odorless dot of paint from its forehead when placed in front of a mirror. If the animal can recognize that the image in the mirror is *itself*, and that itself should not have a dot of paint on its forehead, then the animal is self-aware. End of discussion. And yet I consistently fail to be self-aware in a way that my dog succeeds: once she has marked a tree with her urine she knows it, and doesn't bother urinating on it again. The tree is her mirror, and she smells herself in its glass. I, meanwhile, keep urinating on the same tree.

Even when a philosopher manages to get outside of his mind and into his body for a little while the results are perversely abstract. Peter Singer joined the likes of Jeremy Bentham and Plutarch when he suggested in his 1975 book *Animal Liberation* that the relevant feature of a living being for moral consideration is not its intellect but its capacity to feel pain. In this most animals do not differ very much from us, and thus vegetarianism comes to seem a plausible position indeed. But Singer's basic argument—the most important step is to disabuse us of our "speciesism," our unexamined claim to a special human dignity—lands him, through a series of twists and turns, in bizarre territory: that we are morally justified in killing human infants with hemophilia, or that we should kill one human being to avoid killing 101 chimpanzees. An attempt to recover our fundamental kinship with animals has clearly gone off the rails. Ironically it is that pesky human reason that is to blame: Singer just seems to be *overthinking* it, doesn't he?

All of this philosophizing strikes me as beside the point, and it always has. As a result, when I was a vegetarian, and was asked why I was a vegetarian, I didn't have all that much to say—and that bothered me, because I was supposed to be an intellectual, after all, and intellectuals should be able to justify their actions. There isn't much good in responding to the question with "go read a few novels by J. M. Coetzee." I felt I should be able to explain the nature of my connection to animals somehow or other. At the very least I should try. So I kept trying.

What do we mean when we say that we "stand by" someone, or that we should "be there" for someone? Academic fashion tells us that these are metaphors: their original meaning was physical or spatial, but that meaning became, via a gradual transfer, more and more psychological, figurative instead of literal. Has the literal meaning really been lost, though? One of the most touching things I have ever seen was a simple thing, as simple as one person sitting near another person: a girl sitting through her sister's choir rehearsal. The choir rehearsed in a chapel, and the girl—a twin sister, which is why I noticed in the first place—had set up camp in one of the pews, reading a book and listening to her sister sing. She was roughly college-aged and was in town for a few days; to her it must have just seemed natural to go to her sister's rehearsal, or unnatural not to. A few weeks later I got a visit of my own, from an old friend. When choir night rolled around he didn't come sit in the pews; he drove to another part of the city to run an errand. He told me he needed to "maximize" his time. If I was moved by the twins at first I was even more moved retroactively.

Do you really love someone? The next time she falls asleep in your presence—after sex, say, or if you've been talking late at night—note what it is that you do. Do you get up and go somewhere else? Or do you stay where you are, reading a book maybe, so that you can be there when she wakes up? If I love you, I want to be around you, it's as simple as that. Whatever you are doing, I want to be sitting next to you, and whatever I might be doing, I want you sitting next to me.

My dog obviously feels the same way. I took her to a friend's lake house once, knowing that she would appreciate the water and the walks and the fresh air. The first afternoon I retreated to an upstairs bedroom because I needed to get some work done and couldn't do it downstairs around everyone else and the television. Aggie came upstairs within ten minutes, shoving her muzzle up against the door. When I let her in she looked at me, whimpered, and then turned her body towards the hallway. She then repeated the whole sequence several times: she walked back towards me, she whimpered, she turned towards the door. I could read her loud and clear. When we got downstairs I took a chair in the living room with all the others. Aggie curled up contentedly on the floor and gave me a look that said, more or less: *Don't be ridiculous. You belong here with us.*

Animals are not just proximity experts but experts at body language in general. Your dog can read your body better than you can read hers, because she is reading yours all the time. Chimpanzees failed in their first attempt to learn a human language because they were learning the wrong kind of language; it turns out that chimps don't really have vocal cords suited for speaking—but they do have the bodily awareness to learn sign language. One of the most intriguing details from Jane Goodall's writings about the chimpanzees of Gombe Stream is her description of the courtship gestures the males use to lure females away from the group. If the male doesn't shake that tree branch just right, if he turns away too soon or too abruptly, the female won't follow, and the chance for a rendezvous is lost. Birds dance for courtship too, and bees dance to tell the hive where the good flowers are. Bodily expertise pervades the animal kingdom. We think ourselves above it, but we are wrong—it's more important to us than we are willing or able to admit.

The role that body language plays in human social hierarchy is a known quantity: when Koreans bow, or when a man who cares far too much about weightlifting walks down the street, we see it, and we comment on it. But our bodies don't just stratify us, they bring us together, too. I have long suspected that the "real" reason I am attracted to someone is not the ratio of her waist to her hips or—heaven help us—the symmetry of her face, but rather the way she moves her body. A girlfriend said more or less the same thing to me once: "It's just something about the way you tilt your shoulders." Gaits are important, too; I fell in love with Meg Ryan because of her goofy, boyish walk. Touching is even more important. Hands, for instance, can be bridges, for the passage of electricity, or familiarity, or comfort. If a hand is resting on a shoulder then one thing is known for sure: nothing else is. With the gesture, the one who comforts says to the one who is comforted: *That weight that you think is resting on your shoulders? It's not really there. My hand is.* This is why a hand on the shoulder in the wrong context can be demeaning. The one who gets the pat on the shoulder (or worse, the head) may not need any help, but the patronizing pat implies that he does— and that the patter is the one who can give it to him. This is only indirectly aggressive. But a hand can be plenty aggressive.

There's more than one way to kill an animal. Most of these ways involve a contraption of some kind. Cattle intended for human consumption are generally led single-file to a pen, or "stun box," that can hold them in place while they are stunned by a bolt or an electric shock, after which they are cut open to bleed out. United States law requires that livestock be "rendered insensible to pain" before they are "shackled, hoisted, thrown, cast, or cut," but an exception is made for ritual slaughter, in which the animal dies by "simultaneous and instantaneous severance of the carotid arteries"—in other words, by a cutting of the throat *without* any previous stunning. Even in halal and kosher slaughter, however, the animals are restrained in a box, or with ropes or poles. They must be, so that a clean, swift cut can be delivered. A steer is stronger than a human being, after all. And yet, and yet—there is still that one thing missing. In all those ritual killings, human hands are almost never touching animal bodies.

I have been hunting before; once I shot a rabbit. There is no need to describe it at length, because it wasn't troubling at all. It was exciting. But a gun is a contraption, just like a stun box is. It keeps you at a distance. I can't help feeling that killing something with your bare hands is the real thing, and that using a contraption is a substitute for the complete act—a shorthand. I am fairly sure that the reason I find botched killings so horrifying is that in them we get a glimpse of what the animal would be doing in every killing that is unaided by one of man's clever inventions. The animal would be resisting. And if an animal is resisting, and you are touching that animal, you will be feeling that resistance. The funny thing about the sense of touch, though, is that it goes two ways. One can see without being seen, and hear without being heard, but one cannot touch without being touched back. So if you are touching the animal then it will be touching you too; and its touching will change in response to your touching—which will then change in response to its. Both of you will be revealed as creatures with bodies that respond to the world, creatures with bodies that move, and you will be revealed as such creatures *by each other*. Killing an animal with your bare hands forces you to feel—not to see, but to feel—what you and that animal have in common.

In the end the reason I don't want to kill animals is not that I have made some calculation about the magnitude of pain they feel at death and weighed it against their happiness during life. I often follow the debates in comment sections on the internet, or the more sophisticated versions of those debates from scientists, and all the distinctions leave me cold. They say it is ninety seconds before all the blood drains from the brain of a cow—but they also say it is sixty. They say an animal knows that its fellows are dying behind the doors to the kill floor—but they also say it is blissfully ignorant. The bolt on that stun gun might kill instantaneously—but this might be wishful thinking. The debates aren't entirely irrelevant. They just aren't sufficient. The reason I don't want to kill animals is that the act of killing is itself a bad thing. Put another way, it is not the sort of thing that a human being should be doing. Now, the act of killing is a bad act *because* it is an animal that it is being killed—because the animal is an animal and it feels pain. Of course. But ultimately it is the character of that act itself that is a problem for me.

This helps explain, for example, why the counterargument to vegetarianism that vegetarians often hear misses the mark: that vegetarians are in fact responsible for more animal deaths than meat eaters, because of all the habitat destruction that agriculture requires. In this case, if there is a link between my dietary behavior and the deaths of animals, it is very tenuous. There's just no *me* in that action, as there in fact is if an animal has been slaughtered for my dinner. "You're still ultimately responsible for that habitat destruction." That may be true, but at a certain point my concern for shaping the life I lead outweighs those considerations—the same way my concern for a friend might bring me to perform an act of self-sacrifice that is ultimately to my own detriment, and maybe even his, too. Some acts are just beautiful in themselves, and that's why we do them. And some acts are just ugly in themselves, and that's why we avoid them.

So the animal has lived a long, happy life on that farm full of grass. So what. Go ahead, let all the various arguments and counterarguments have their place. Yes, I do think that humans are more important than animals. Yes, it might be different if the animal dies a natural death. And so on and so on. But in the complexity of moral reckoning, the ugliness of the act of killing still has for me a kind of sovereignty that is hard to overcome. I just don't want to use the same hand I use to bless to restrain—to kill something that lives and breathes and fights, just like I do.

A S YOU CAN see, I've gotten myself into quite a bind. After a lot of self-experimentation, and some support from tribes and peoples past, I think I finally know how I need to eat. In particular, I know that it is better for me to eat meat than not to eat it. Not just because I like the taste, or because it is convenient, but because without it I am significantly worse off—so much so, in fact, that when I abstain from meat I feel I am denying my nature, or denying myself the opportunity to fully become what I truly am. On the other hand, I do not want to kill. And not just because I find it unpleasant—I have the strength to do what is unpleasant—but because I think it is morally wrong. I think that in killing animals I deny my ethical being essentially, or at least strain it considerably. Either way, the killing is bad—the highest level of bad.

It appears to me that most people do not have this problem, or at least they don't claim to. Ethical vegetarians, for one, tend to believe that the ethical way to eat is also the healthy way to eat. This is not surprising, because our health care professionals and our media believe it is healthy, too. Vegetarians often go further: the health they have in mind is not just humdrum bodily health, the firing of the cylinders and the meshing of the gears, but a spiritual health, a holistic well-being. I read my fair share of pro-vegetarian books in my day— borrowed from fellow co-op eaters usually—and they made sense to me: meat imparts negative energy to the one who eats it; meat weighs you down; switching to a vegetarian diet makes your spirit *lighter*. Thoreau has something very similar to say in *Walden* (even if he does recommend hunting to young boys): "I believe that every man who has ever been earnest to preserve his higher or poetic faculties in the best condition has been particularly inclined to abstain from animal food." The physical harm that meat causes the body does not end in the body: it reaches up into the spirit.

On the other side of the coin one finds the same harmony of ideals, just inverted. Meat eaters who believe that eating meat is essential to health usually have some kind of ethical account to go alongside their dietary preference (when they are bothering to think about it at all, that is). One option available, of course, is the classic route: the simple dismissal that animals have any rights or feelings or importance whatsoever—or, expressed positively, a firm belief in the uniqueness of human dignity. With the new generation of "foodies" new modes of justification have arrived, which enlarge the palette a bit. There are a handful of guidelines for eating "humanely," but foremost among these is the vaguely Michael Pollan-inspired idea that we should be "connected" to our food. In 2011, Facebook founder Mark Zuckerberg got connected to his food in a major way when he resolved to spend an entire year eating meat only from animals he had killed himself. Inspirational to the Zuckerbergian enterprise, surely, was the assumption that the born farmers and the seasoned hunters of the world are close to nature in a way that we hysterical urbanites are not. They must, then, be in the right.

The justifications of the meat eaters run even deeper. Every now and then someone on a paleo blog suggests that we say a prayer before eating meat, and hunters debate in forums about whether or not we should be performing Native American rituals over fresh kills. The unifying idea seems to be that the animal died for us; as a result we give thanks. For many self-aware meat eaters, this respect for the animal after its death is just part of a larger, more spiritual conception. Nature is a circle: death is a part of life, and we humans may kill now, but eventually we will in turn be food for the universe. Lierre Keith, an author whom paleos and ancestrals do not read much of anymore because of her unsavory anarchist views, expressed this conception with some elegance in

Kate MacDowell, *Casualty*, 2009

her 2009 book *The Vegetarian Myth*. She tells of how she was comforted, in her conversion to meat eating, by a nineteenth-century anecdote about an apple tree in Rhode Island: the tree's roots had snaked their way into some human graves, wrapping themselves around the remains of the bodies and taking the bones for the tree's own nourishment. This returning of the favor does seem like a kind of justice, and we can imagine extending that justice indefinitely: perhaps that apple tree made an apple from the minerals in those bones; and perhaps some animal ate that apple; and then deposited the seeds in its droppings somewhere far away; and one of those seeds grew into another tree ... which wrapped its roots around another human being. And on and on, maybe. The circle is eternity's favorite shape.

Ethical, healthy vegetarians; and ethical, healthy meat eaters. People who think about what they eat fall into one of these two camps with a suspicious regularity. I can safely say that I have never met an ethical vegetarian who thought he was significantly damaging his health by abstaining from meat; and I have never met a health-conscious meat eater who did not have an account ready to justify his meat consumption (or didn't reach for one when challenged). I have even seen, several times, vegetarians convert to an ancestral diet and adopt within weeks a new ethics to go along with their new diet, as if ideas were merely superficial, mere tools the body uses to placate the mind—a phenomenon it will no doubt delight philosophical materialists to hear about. (It should also come as no surprise that the new meat eaters have an account for the *environmental* superiority of an omnivorous diet, too.) Why does it seem so difficult not to fall into one of the two camps? Why can't we be vegetarians and also believe that we are denying our own nature, like a lion eating a salad? Why can't we be meat eaters and also believe that we are terrible people, like a person who can't restrain his desire to molest children, even though he knows it's wrong? Consider the following hypothetical confession from a vegetarian: "I just cannot live with myself if I kill animals, and that is why I don't eat meat. On the other hand, I also think that I am denying my nature. I think that I was designed to eat meat, like the lion, but I choose to ignore this, and as a result I am frail." Why is it so unlikely that we would ever hear such a confession?

This question, although it may not seem so at first, is a deep one. It is one version of a question that human beings have been asking for a very long time. We don't think about it when we talk about food, usually—but we could. And we probably should.

III

THE LISBON EARTHQUAKE of November 1, 1755 was to eighteenth-century Europe a bit like the attacks of September 11, 2001 have been to twenty-first-century America. It was not just the sheer loss of life that caused the shock in each case—if comparing numbers means anything at all, the Portuguese had it much worse, as tens of thousands were wiped out—but the gory details of each tragedy. In 1755 Europeans were horrified to hear that human beings had met their ends trapped under the rubble of multistory buildings: alone, in the dark, probably an arm or leg pinned to the ground. Many suffered that particular fate on September 11th as well, although dying under a building seems tame by September 11th standards. Few of us will be able to forget watching those who chose to jump instead of burn—a death that no Hollywood screenwriter had ever managed to concoct for his characters.

November 1st brought out the intellectuals too, just like September 11th. But if the God talk was marginalized after 9/11, it was in the very center of the discourse after Lisbon. And not just because people were more likely to talk about God in the eighteenth century. The earthquake, after all, had not been caused by human beings flying airplanes; and not only were tall buildings destroyed, but churches too. There were no people to blame for the evil. God himself, it seemed, had destroyed his places of worship, not to mention his creatures worshipping inside.

Before the year was through, Voltaire—playwright, essayist, man of reason—had anonymously circulated a poem on the earthquake, with the full title "Poem on the Lisbon Disaster; Or an Examination of the Axiom 'All is Well.'" All was not well, obviously, and that was Voltaire's point. Voltaire's particular target was the "theodicy" of Alexander Pope and Gottfried Wilhelm Leibniz: in brief, their attempt to justify the existence of evil in the world as necessary for the greater good that God has in mind. Voltaire would eventually come to attack this idea with humor a few years later in *Candide*—the protagonist's Leibnizian tutor Pangloss proclaims this world "the best of all possible worlds" while parts of his syphilitic body fall off—but in the poem on Lisbon Voltaire simply lets his frustration flow onto the page. Was there some reason that Lisbon was punished, rather than London, Paris or Madrid? Was there more sin in Lisbon? Did the good of the whole really require such a loss of life? Would the universe be worse off without swallowing up Lisbon? Voltaire does not claim the existence of God rules out all particular evils—if it did the human propensity for toothaches would have extinguished religious belief long ago. But at a certain point, with a certain mass of needless suffering, the balance tips and the fundamental goodness of the universe comes very much into question.

In August of the following year, Jean-Jacques Rousseau—already famous, but less famous, and considerably younger, than Voltaire—sent a nice long letter to the author of the *Poème sur le désastre de Lisbonne*, respectfully arguing the opposite position. Rousseau's gambit was on its surface fairly cheeky, but his intent was serious: the real problem with the Lisbon earthquake, Rousseau suggested, was not the earthquake itself, but the fact that men had built such large buildings for themselves in the first place. If they hadn't built the buildings, they wouldn't have been buried under them. Living in the woods, in huts or tents, families would simply have stepped outside when the earth started shaking; and if their huts had been destroyed they would have walked a few miles away and built new ones. To the question often posed in the aftermath of the earthquake—"Why, oh why, couldn't it have happened in the middle of the wilderness instead?"—Rousseau answered that it probably *had* happened in the wilderness, many times. We just never heard about it; which proved Rousseau's point.

Not too long before the letter to Voltaire, Rousseau had published his *Discourse on the Origin of Inequality*, which was filled with the kinds of thoughts about human prehistory that would lead someone to make the kind of suggestion about the earthquake that Rousseau did. Man in his natural state, according to Rousseau, was solitary, peaceful and happy. Drifting through his environment without cares, he rarely did anything other than "sate his hunger beneath an oak, slake his thirst at the first stream, and find his bed at the foot of the same tree that supplied his meal." If male and female human beings happened to run into each other in the woods, they would mate, and if there was a child then there was a child—but as soon as the child could survive on his own the mother unceremoniously sent him packing. There was never reason to quarrel: if someone stole your meal, you could just find another one; and no one could steal your property, because there was no such thing as property. All was well. Sadly it did not end well: Rousseau had a story to tell, and that story was not pleasant. From this original, blissful state of affairs, man tumbled into a gradual, painful decline. With the arrival of families and huts, human beings still had it pretty good; but after the huts came agriculture, and then fences, and then rich and poor, and then politics, and then oppression. Before long, we had stumbled into the tyrannical world we live in today—where, in Rousseau's grim vision, we all demean ourselves, we all profit at each other's expense, and we all wish, secretly or not-so-secretly, to cut every throat until the earth belongs to us.

If there is a phrase that will be forever associated with Rousseau—like Thomas Hobbes's "nasty, brutish and short" or Nietzsche's "God is dead"—it is "the noble savage." Rousseau did love his noble savages, but he never used the exact phrase "noble savage"; more important, he never once told us to try to *become* noble savages. Rousseau was not exactly offering advice when he described those hypothetical primitives living in the woods, immune to the earth's shaking; true, he probably would not have opposed a resolution to build smaller houses in Lisbon, but he certainly would have opposed a mass egress into the wilderness. We tend to agree with him. Of the untold millions who have either read Rousseau's book or felt its influence indirectly, precious few have actually destroyed their credit cards and walked into the woods. And yet we love the book and we love its story; we love that noble, primitive fellow sitting under the oak tree. Our imagination just keeps coming back to him. Why?

One nice thing about Rousseau's story is that it is not an inevitable one: the series of steps that carried us from innocence to corruption were not, strictly speaking, *necessary*; they could have gone another way. And if we were once originally good, and things could have gone another way in the past, then they might still be able to go another way in the future—the way of justice, perhaps, instead of the way of tyranny. And so Rousseau is the first sociologist, or the first critical theorist; before Marx, before Adorno, he gave us reason to hope that modernity could be escaped. Yet there is something even more reassuring about Rousseau's story. In the state of nature man fits perfectly with his environment, and he is at peace. The desires and fears that lead to despair and conflict simply aren't there for him—or if they are then his environment keeps him from getting into too much trouble, like a baby-proofed house. And indeed every time Rousseau senses a potential objection about his primitive man, some disjunction or awkwardness or contradiction, something else slides into place to meet the need: Will primitive man not be helpless in the woods without tools? No; he is stronger than we are because he hasn't been relying on those very tools his whole life. Is he not tormented by sexual desire? Not at all, because for him the desire only arises when the provocation is present. Will he not die? He will, but he doesn't fear death; he doesn't even really know what it is.

We might balk at the details of Rousseau's portrait, and they are often outlandish—it becomes clear in the footnotes that Rousseau thought the orangutans of southeast Asia were actually primitive men—but most of us probably do carry around with us a conception of human nature that more or less resembles Rousseau's. We think that we are out of joint with our world, and that it is a messy place, filled with greed and competition and cell phones and global warming; but we also assume that if things were the way they should be, then the world would be simpler, and we would be fundamentally at peace with it and with ourselves. And we find this thought comforting, just as Rousseau does. Even if the modern world is full of conflict, at least we know that when things are the way they're supposed to be then there is no conflict. At least we know that *in our nature* there is no conflict. This is the self-conception we have inherited from Rousseau: the world is messy, "the system" is messy, culture is messy, history is messy—but *we* are not messy, at least not when we are what we should be. Rousseau projects this state of nature—this condition in which everything is as it should be—into the past, as do we generally, thanks to our history books. But that which is behind us is also our nature, and in our nature we are at peace. For Voltaire the Lisbon earthquake proved that the universe is inherently inhospitable, inherently screwed up. Rousseau's idea turned Voltaire's on its head: the universe is inherently welcoming, and not inhospitable—*we're* the ones who have screwed things up.

Ideas like these, ideas that we carry around with us everywhere we go, tend to be very powerful. They can dictate the way we love, the way we fight, the way we die. They can even dictate—the way we eat. When a vegetarian thinks that in not killing animals he is obeying his nature, and *also* thinks that in keeping flesh out of his belly he is obeying his nature (by doing what is healthy), it is rare that he has come to those two views separately, as if through an impartial process of experimentation. He holds those two views together because he assumes, with Rousseau, that our nature is harmonious, that in our nature we are at peace. The new ancestral dieter, the ethical omnivore, is no different. It may seem that a natural world in which humans kill animals for food is not a world in which humans are at peace. But the ethical omnivore thinks that the killing of animals, just like the eating of meat, is natural; and therefore there is no conflict in his soul. The Rousseauian assumption tyrannizes his thought, even if he doesn't realize it: if eating meat is healthiest, if it is proper to our nature, then certainly it *must* also be true that there is nothing about our nature that forbids killing. With the one comes the other, sure as the sun shines. That is the power of the idea.

And indeed, how could things possibly be otherwise? What kind of a world would that be in which we were asked to abstain from the food that we need in order to be what we are? What kind of a world would that be in which feeding ourselves required us to do what our very being tells us not to? Somehow, for some reason, that just seems *wrong*. But why do we assume this? Why are we all Rousseauians? Just because life would be unpleasant if we weren't?

There is in fact another way of thinking about things. Because it is repellent it usually remains inaccessible to us. Every once in a while, though, we catch a glimpse of it—when we are distraught, when something about the world seems infuriating, or when life seems impossible.

n+1 magazine / **a journal of**
literature,   culture,   and   politics
published   three   times   a   year.
s   u   b   s   c   r   i   b   e
for   complete   online   access:
w w w . n p l u s o n e m a g . c o m

IN THE HISTORY of philosophy this other way of thinking generally goes by the name of "pessimism." It too leads a sort of underground existence, from time to time erupting into the philosophical mainstream, the occasional wretched mood of an otherwise cheery discipline. (Pessimism is probably more common in literature and the arts, where it is known as "the tragic world-view"—ancient Greek and Shakespearian tragedy being two of its favorite haunts.) Other than Arthur Schopenhauer, there are no prominent examples of philosophers who made a career out of the topic. Pessimism exists more as a rare exception within a philosopher's oeuvre: an essay from Emerson, an aphorism from Nietzsche, a poem from Voltaire. Or it exists as a mere conceptual possibility, something hiding behind one's thought, or perhaps, more insidiously, something repressed beneath it.

The term itself is not used in the philosophical tradition the way it is used in everyday speech, where it usually refers to a negative attitude about the future in particular. It denotes rather a negative evaluation of *everything*. But pessimism is not just a contingent judgment about that everything. Pessimism doesn't just say "hey, things are bad," or "life is rough." These sound a little too accidental—as if things might not have been bad, or life might not have been rough. In the pessimistic worldview, life is *essentially* rough. So perhaps something more like: "In this world nothing is certain, except death and taxes" or "life's a bitch and then you die." Though even these don't quite hit the mark, because pessimism is a *particular* way of understanding what it means for life to be—pardon me—a bitch. In its best form, pessimism says something about the relationship between man and his world, something beyond the simple claim that our pleasures are outweighed by our pains. Pessimism takes a wide perspective.

Consider the universe for a moment. It is big. It has matter in it, and light. There are a few laws that govern what goes on within its confines: one of them is gravity, which is a handy organizational device, keeping matter together, keeping things revolving around other things. In addition to ice and heat and rocks there are some plants and animals, too. They grow on their own and move on their own, but they don't make much trouble. Everything is part of the big mechanism: the big clock with its intricate, intertwined parts. The sun lies over the waves; the big fish eat the little fish; the ocean sends its water up to the clouds. Everything is harmonious and tidy. Beautiful, even.

Now ask yourself: If there were no human beings, would something be missing? Isn't the universe complete without them? Do we really need a creature in the universe that is *aware* of the universe and not just a part of it? If it were only a matter of awareness, the human situation would not be quite so odd; but this very aware creature is also very temporary. It can produce other creatures just like itself by sloughing off some of its own cells, sure, but it comes with an

Kate MacDowell, *Predator*, 2009

expiration date, and it knows that, and, with any honesty, it feels that every day of its adult life. This odd little creature is capable of contemplating the beauty of the universe around it, and can make beautiful things of its own, and can think about how much more special it is than the other creatures, and can imagine what it would be like to live in the universe forever—but it nevertheless dies. Does the universe really need a creature like this? Because it seems like a cruel joke. The victim of the joke has been given just enough capacity to appreciate and treasure what it will never have: here is, *ha ha ha*, the very recipe of frustration. If you want to recreate the human situation, throw your kids in the car and drive them to the amusement park, talking to them all the while about how glorious it is—and then turn around at the entrance. You could recreate the human situation this way, but there's no need. We're all living it.

Science, in an act of boldness, declares: "The universe doesn't care about us." The religious are just telling themselves comforting lies, we are told; only science has the courage to recognize the truth and accept it. And the truth, obviously, is that the universe is perfectly neutral with respect to human beings. It lets be what will be—sometimes things turn out well, sometimes they don't. But science, and we the scientific, have neglected a third alternative: that the universe might be neither good nor neutral, but distinctly *bad*. Not *intentionally* bad, mind you—the thought that a deity is intentionally harming us would make the world a *kinder* place, ultimately, because we would assume we were being punished for a reason, which would be a sort of comfort. In the pessimistic view, even this last-ditch appeal to goodness is impermissible. The world is, to the contrary, just essentially, deeply bad. We simply are in a horrific position. Full stop.

Even just grasping the thought is difficult, because we are so accustomed to thinking otherwise. "It couldn't possibly be that way." Why not? "A situation like that just couldn't..." Just couldn't what? The mind seizes up at the thought, just as it did when we were kids and tried to think about what was outside the universe. When we were kids it was fun, though; now, it's just nauseating. This, the tragic vision, might be false, or maybe it's just the way that a bunch of depressed people have tried to ruin the world for the rest of us. But, you have to admit, there are some pretty compelling reasons to live in denial of it—which makes you wonder once again if it is true, and if life and culture and everything else are just part of a great conspiracy to shush the whole thing up.

Death is not the only frustration. There are others that the tragic mode can uncover, to reveal the world in its darkness. Human beings, for example, tend to want things that are fundamentally at odds with each other. And not just little things—humans generally find a way to persevere even if they don't have time for *both* a manicure *and* a haircut. Much deeper contradictions are sown into them, contradictions that plague them for a lifetime, even if they are reluctant to admit it. Take sex, for example. There is a tension in the love life of the American male so widespread that it has become a part of our cultural subconscious, breaking free in comedy routines, self-help books, and good old-fashioned common sense: the difficult choice between the intimacy of monogamy and the novelty and variety of the single life. Men who are in relationships yearn to be single, and men who are single yearn to be in relationships (although men are less likely to admit the latter to other men). What is remarkable about the tension is not its mere existence—that is, again, a bit of common sense. What is remarkable about the tension is both that it is incredibly powerful, and that we are just as incredibly reluctant to admit to its power. Men often destroy their lives in the pursuit of extramarital affairs. And while in the movies the woman who tempts the husband away is normally gorgeous, a younger version of the wife (why else would he cheat?), in the real world men routinely throw their lives away for women they would otherwise not be attracted to. It is uncomfortable to think about, because it shows just how strong the pull of novelty is, and hints at the numbing revulsion the husband must feel for his wife—his wife whom he loves and respects. The tension is so uncomfortable that it gets swept under the carpet whenever it can. Just look at the sex scandals of American politics, which send us all scurrying after carpets. Conservatives, in their clamor for resignations, imply that the one who succumbs to lust is a mere aberration, thus reassuring themselves that the internal struggle is nonexistent for the "normal" man, or the "good" man. The soccer-viewing classes get in on the cover-up as well, with their reminder that the Europeans are laughing at us for our prudery—if only we could let go of our puritanism, then everything would be just fine! We act as if it is only ignorance or luck that keeps us from the solution. But there is no solution.

Social life has more dilemmas in store, and we meet them with equally misplaced confidence. Each of us has developed a strategy, hard won, for dealing with other human beings. Some incline toward toughness; others toward trust. Whatever the strategy, all are certain that theirs is right, and all are certain that everyone else's, consequently, is wrong. (To paraphrase Thomas Hobbes: we might be willing to admit that other people are more musical or funnier or better at math, but we know we are wiser.) This is a reflection on human vanity. This is also a reflection on human arrogance. For when we think that we are right and everyone else is wrong, we think that there *is* such a thing as right— and there is no such thing as right, at least not when it comes to other human beings. No matter how suave the social strategy, it will fail, again and again. A thick, Darwinian skin not only keeps love out, it is also tiring to maintain: the dictator sleeps with one eye open. A confidence in human goodness, even if cautious, will still be taken advantage of from time to time. "You have to open

yourself up! You can't be afraid to get hurt again!" True, but you *will* get hurt again, eventually.

Hope is a nice thing to have. It makes sense that it is our default setting, that most of us carry around the comforting assumptions we do: that we can love without complication, that death is something that happens to other people, that we belong on our earth. It makes sense, too, that the history of philosophy is a nearly unbroken chain of attempts to hope in just the right way, from Plato's glittering world of Forms all the way to Hegel's End of History. It makes even more sense that there is such a thing as religion. If all philosophical systems are covert ploys for salvation—and they are—then all religions are overt ones. Faith is the ultimate optimism. It is an assertion that the universe is benevolent and not ruthless, that we belong here, that life is not a nightmare, and, even if it is, then at least we will wake up from it in a world where all the contradictions of life are resolved; in short, it is an assertion that everything, eventually, will be OK. Jean-Jacques Rousseau believed in God. But he also gave us moderns our secular version of optimism, when he told us about that serene and satisfied primitive, at home in the woods. In Rousseau's work, one kind of belief that everything will be OK was making way for another: Christ was making way for the man under the oak tree. Our new, secular optimism, in other words, is a replacement for our old, Christian optimism.

Every comforting assumption we have about human nature, then, every automatic thought that hides the contradictions of life from view—every one of these serves the same purpose that religion does. Every one is, essentially, a god. The sexually "healthy" male is a god. The perfect marriage is a god. The perfect social strategy is a god, too, along with its companion deities, the twin theories of absolute human goodness and absolute human evil. Contemporary politics also provides a nice selection of gods: the Bumper Sticker, for example—whether Prius or domestic pickup truck—rests assured in the belief that all of our problems are caused by our refusal to accept the Bumper Sticker's gospel, and not by deep, irresolvable tensions endemic to human coexistence. (The intellectual's Bumper Sticker? Hegel.) On and on it goes, from one part of our life to another. How would we get by without our pantheon of gods? They make everything easier. It is no wonder that pessimism is unpopular.

THERE IS A saying I learned from my mother, one of those jokey bits of folk wisdom that I am not particularly good at heeding. "You should never talk about religion or politics at the dinner table." Short and sweet—and insightful, too. But this jokey bit of folk wisdom threatens to become jokey in an annoyingly cute kind of way, because now there's another thing we can't talk about at the dinner table: dinner. With a fluff piece here and a cartoon there, our high-end media outlets are beginning, with small steps, to make us uncomfortably aware that food has become a religious affair. Not that religion chooses to express itself in and through food—that has always been the case. Rather that our attitudes about food have *themselves* become religious. The surest external sign of this is the general, pervasive craze around dining: chefs are all of a sudden celebrities (and for some reason we want them to talk, not just cook); and the culinary art has become virtually everyone's hobby, the newest way to show off (instead of expertise in jazz, say, or interior decorating). But these are, ultimately, symptoms: the heart of the matter is that an increasing number of us seek our very *identity*, or a goodly share of it, in food. For the food-devout among us a diet is not just a way of eating, but a way of life. And because an identity, in telling you who you are, also tells you who you are not, the internet food-o-sphere is becoming a pretty violent place. The comment sections on food blogs are like quicksand: the more you struggle, the more you get stuck—until someone pulls you out to take the kids to school or mow the lawn. Anger is addictive. Especially religious anger.

If the ancestrals are onto something about health, and the vegetarians are onto something about the evil of killing animals, then we finally have a method for all the madness. Why have we gotten so worked up about food? Because food forces us to call on our gods. Every dietary creed is a way of addressing—denying, or covering up, or rationalizing away—a particularly disturbing contradiction: that, on the one hand, we need to eat animals, but, on the other hand, killing animals is inhumane. Mind you, the absolute truth of these two propositions is not required; only the suspicion of their truth. Meat might be healthy; and killing might be wrong. This is the dilemma. What is at stake in it is what is at stake in all the fundamental human dilemmas: our very sense that we are *at home* in the world. If we find harmony with ourselves in our world, then it can feel like home. If our home requires us to make impossible choices—the animal-loving meat eater sacrificing his ethics, or the animal-loving vegetarian sacrificing his health—then it cannot be much of a home. We do not want to live without a home, so we do what we must: we create our food gods to wish away the problem of food, just as we created our gods of romance and politics to wish away the problems they brought along.

Conditions are ripe for food religion. But maybe it was only a matter of time before we needed to get religious about food anyway. Because the new food religions have to deal with something our old religions did not: an unavoidable omnipresence. It is possible to go to God only twice a year—Easter and

Christmas—or thrice a lifetime—for "hatching, matching and dispatching," as the saying has it. It is possible, especially in the United States, to ignore politics. And it is possible to swear off love, for months, or years, or decades—whatever it takes. But there's no getting away from food. You eat it, or you die. Our growing awareness of the problem of animals, then, is right up under our noses. It won't be going anywhere anytime soon.

A T THE FIRST annual Ancestral Health Symposium, in 2011, one of the speakers—Denise Minger, herself a former vegan—asked if there were any former vegetarians or vegans in attendance. Half of the audience raised their hands. I laugh at myself whenever I think of this. Not too long ago I was as vegetarian as one could be, in thought, word and deed; now I am a true-believing member of the "ancestral community." Maybe we all just need something to belong to, *some* religion or other—and it doesn't really matter which one.

We do have to choose, after all. Life is pretty much impossible without choosing one direction over another—we would starve at the crossroads if we didn't. And life is pretty much impossible without giving ourselves convincing reasons for choosing as we do, even when no choice is a good one. If we were steadily plagued by a visceral, overwhelming awareness of our human condition—our dilemmas, our deaths, the precariousness of our choices—we would be paralyzed. You cannot stare tragedy in the face for very long.

So why look at all then? Why not just rest cozy in whatever religion you've found? Well, the tragic worldview does bring with it one conspicuous blessing: sympathy for other human beings. And that's something we could use more of, at our contentious dinner parties, and on our contentious internet. The silver lining of tragedy is that it belongs to all of us. If we are all subject to the same tragedies, the same ineliminable contradictions, then we see other people not as dullards who haven't managed to find the perfect solutions we have; we see them as fellow sufferers. Fellow sufferers, and fellow travelers, too—for we are all dealing with the same problems, even if we are dealing with them differently. If we keep a little tragedy in our minds we can welcome others into our homes. We can break bread together. We can say, at the very least: I understand you.

symposium
what is privacy for?

Amanda Greavette, *It's a Human Thing (It's a Girl? It's a Girl!)*, 2007

INTO THE CAVE

by Dawn Herrera-Helphand

Like many women with countercultural affinities and too much education, when I got pregnant I began planning for a "natural," i.e. drug-free, childbirth. Considering that up to that point I had greatly enjoyed the medical, reproductive and recreational benefits of pharmaceutical drugs, some might find my choice to forego them in this particular pain-racked enterprise a bit ridiculous—yet a consistent logic motivated the decision. After all, there are only so many edge experiences an adult can responsibly pursue. Against the statistical odds I went through with it, and came away from the labor with a bright-eyed newborn, busted capillaries around my own eyes, and a deeper sense of how privacy enables us to experience bodily life in its fullness.

•

When Hannah Arendt's *The Human Condition* was published in 1959, the second wave of feminism was wind blowing across the water of American life—an energy that was gathering and palpable, if largely invisible. In the decades that followed, however, Arendt was largely indifferent to the politics of gender and sex. She refused outright to define her intellectual project in terms of her gender, and certain arguments, even her general view of social and political life, have been criticized as antithetical to feminist concerns.

In *The Human Condition*, Arendt argues that some activities are fit to appear to other people, and others not; some belong in public and others in private. The public is, or ought to be, the bright realm of free speech and action, the place of politics proper. Being seen, people and actions are properly open to judgment by others, so as to allow us to decide issues pertinent to our life in common. By contrast, the private is the shadow realm of necessity, where we labor to maintain our bodies and the life of our species. While human actions constitute history in linear time, our unending labor for biological maintenance swings in a circle, a ceaseless cycle.

This cycle and woman have been defined in terms of one another. Arendt alludes to this fact—she associates women's emancipation with modernity's diminished concern for hiding bodily functions, for example—but does not question, or even really pause over it. And her implicit argument that what has traditionally been called "women's work" should properly remain hidden and unseen is sharply at odds with the feminist demand that women's activities be made visible, so as to be justly valued and compensated. In her attempt to puzzle through the question of women's work in contemporary life, Adrienne Rich turned to Arendt for guidance and found instead precisely the thinking that she sought to oppose. *The Human Condition*, Rich wrote, was "a lofty and crippled book" conceived by a "female mind nourished on male ideology."

I am a feminist, and I love Arendt's work. Still, those claims about labor and the body have stuck in my craw since I first read her books as an undergraduate. A decade of turning and returning to *The Human Condition* didn't help me square my view that the labor that sustains bodily life ought to be valued, and must therefore be seen, with Arendt's claim that this labor wants, even *demands*, to be done in private.

•

Arendt calls the private realm "the realm of necessity." The language is hers, but it's a variation on an old binary theme, the song of necessity and freedom. Figured variously as chaos, the animal, the feminine and the shadow realm, human necessity is the umbrella term for those aspects of life not subject to the rational will. In Arendt's understanding, it especially signifies the immediate reality of embodied life, the thick stuff of it, the part that's been squicking out Western squares from Plato to the present. To the chagrin of the Platonist, it is an irreducible aspect of our living being.

In its most mundane iterations, necessity is a driving and an equalizing force that compels everyone. We all eat and drink, we shit, we sleep and probably try to get off—you, yes you. With luck, the resources for doing so are reasonably secure and we can meet these demands with dignity, securely and without fear of opprobrium at the salience of our appetites and drives. Fussing over particulars aside, there is not a lot of room for reason-giving or reason-having in this realm of experience. Bodies drive us in some things. We do them because we are essentially beholden—we have to. And, having to do them, we prefer to do them in private.

Pain is the most intense manifestation of this phenomenon. As Elaine Scarry puts it in *The Body in Pain* (1985), pain brings about "a state anterior to language, to the sounds and cries a human being makes before language is learned." Scarry links pain's destruction of language to the fact that, unlike most states of consciousness, it has no reference point—in pain, the whole of the matter is bounded in the body of who feels it. Pain is not an experience that can be shared in such a way that its full force will be adequately communicated to another. It is in this sense a private phenomenon. No accident that, absent some cause that would render it meaningful, one prefers to suffer pain out of public view.

•

Privacy shelters us as we suffer and also take pleasure in physical life. It is difficult, and probably futile, to parse how much of this is "natural" and how much the product of cultural sedimentation. A number of artists have tested this boundary through willful public performances of necessity. John and Yoko's "Bed-In," the work of Tracey Emin, and a bowl-cut artist (name lost to the flow of culture) who recently lived for weeks in a hamster-house museum exhibit come to mind.

The best example of polemical public privacy, though, is perhaps the oldest: Diogenes of Sinope. Diogenes, who lived in the fifth century BCE, was an originator of Cynic philosophy. Ancient Cynicism had little in common with the pessimistic apathy that we associate with the word today. Rather, it ruthlessly questioned calcified proprieties and mocked the stricture of truths that occlude living and thinking freely. Diogenes is a kind of trickster figure of ancient philosophy, insulting Alexander the Great, eating in the marketplace, masturbating in the marketplace, concluding a well-received

Amanda Greavette, *Ring the bells that can still ring, Forget your perfect offering, There is a crack in everything, That's how the light gets in*, 2010

lecture by squatting and taking a shit. Michel Foucault devoted his final lecture course to analyzing Diogenes' philosophical strategy of *scandalia*, from the Greek for stumbling block. The Cynic became, in himself, a stumbling block to the lethargic corruption of business as usual.

Diogenes' cheerful performances used necessity to assert autonomy over the crushing pressure of arbitrary and stultifying mores. By willfully publicizing his bodily functions, he changed what it meant for these necessary activities to be exposed, asserting his dignity as a fact that did not depend on the judgment of others.

•

Being beholden to necessity is not essentially gendered—men eat, sleep, shit, orgasm and get sick, and, generally, they prefer to do it out of view of others.

We all attend to the business of managing necessity every day, but some events in the course of a life are intensely shot through with it. The most obvious is death, or rather being at the edge of death, when life makes itself known through its impending cessation—or so I would imagine. I know from experience, however, that serious illness or accident also turns the body itself into a scandal, driving your attention to its bare need. Old age perhaps imposes this condition by gentle degrees.

Natural childbirth, though, is an experience of the necessity of human life par excellence. Unlike many other experiences where necessity is felt in its full driving force, giving birth can be lived as something other than a trauma or decline. Necessity can be experienced as an *event*—an out-of-the-ordinary occurrence with the potential to restructure one's world.

In the not-too-distant past, to experience this event full-throttle was not an option most American women could choose. In a 1939 *Atlantic Monthly* article entitled "I Had a Baby," Lenore Pelham Friedrich described the "unpleasant, upsetting and baffling experience" of being fully anesthetized for the birth of her first three children:

> With the first ones, gas and ether were used. I experienced the sensation which has always seemed to me worse than any pain—of struggling for consciousness, going down into blackness, coming up only to know that something big and dreadful is happening, to feel fear, to hear oneself moaning, to sense strange people, with offensive professional voices; then to go way under, and to recover hours later, clean and dizzy, in a strange bed, and be told that a boy has been had.

When Friedrich asked her regular OB to deliver her fourth child without anesthesia he refused her with the words, "I don't like to see people suffer."

This childbirth scenario will be familiar to anyone who watched Betty Draper's terrifying Demerol head-trip on the third season of *Mad Men*. There was no medical rationale for general anesthesia, which was not routinely practiced in Europe. The laboring woman was made into what Friedrich called a "sterilized package, babbling and unaware," at the discretion of a wholly male class of professional physicians. The exclusion of women from the process is sad but not surprising, given the modern history of medicine. In *Witches, Midwives and Nurses*

(1973), Barbara Ehrenreich and Deirdre English show how midwifery was discredited and outlawed to justify the professionalization of relatively untrained male obstetricians in nineteenth-century America. With the notable exception of witch burnings, this history mirrors the early modern European replacement of female village healers with church-endorsed male doctors who relied primarily on humorism and bloodletting. The predictable consequences for women's authority with respect to the birth process are still palpable in many American hospitals, though this history was largely unknown until Ehrenreich and English's self-published "booklet" went viral, helping to kindle the midwifery movement.

Lenore Pelham Friedrich wanted to know what labor was like, so she went to Switzerland to deliver her baby awake. Wanting the same, I was able to have mine in a hospital with a midwifery practice. The severe congenital defect that I was born with, my driving distance from an ER and the fact that it was my first child, all made the comfort of a home birth seem too risky. Thanks to decades of feminist political and medical advocacy, some hospitals now offer integrated OB/GYN-midwifery practices, where delivery without epidural is supported, or at least not discouraged. If not strictly the *best* of both worlds, I reasoned, we'll at least get their essentials.

I must pause to emphasize the deeply personal nature of decisions over where and how to labor. Here, the legal sense of "privacy" that protects the right to terminate a pregnancy by ever-narrower margins becomes germane. I have a lot of reasons for my decisions, and I think they are good reasons. But they are good *for me*, and this does not imply that they are good for you.

They are private, not public, reasons. In other words, this experience is not, except *perhaps* in extremis, open to the judgment of others. Legal privacy shelters from public intervention as literal privacy shelters from public view. The absolute necessity that characterizes the birth of a child makes clear the absolute freedom every woman ought to have in her decision to bear one.

•

The most beautiful account of childbirth I've encountered in prose is the closing scene of Meridel Le Sueur's underground feminist classic *The Girl*. Written at the tail end of the Depression but not published until 1978, the novel is a fictionalized account of events drawn from the lives of the women in Le Sueur's writing group. It combines a potboiler plot with radical political commentary and bleeding-edge representations of how it feels to be alive, all in a colloquial vernacular that occasionally rises to the level of poetry. In the closing scene, the nameless title character enters the final throes of labor in a makeshift tenement where a public demonstration is also being organized. The women, says the girl, "made a little cave in the corner." Then, as she begins to push, "It's the realest dream."

Through most of my own long labor I made a show of autonomy. I joked with my mother and husband, negotiated the terms of medical intervention with hospital staff, and balanced my body over the rolling waves of pain—between "How could it be worse?" and "Is that all there is?"

As the moment drew near, though, this performance of control diminished to

Amanda Greavette, *The Balm*, 2013

a vanishing point. I requested a Coca-Cola. My rational will drew itself up and moved aside as I felt the force of life itself flow down and through my body, like water falling from a great height. They made a kind of cave around me. I screamed and was gently admonished to move the sound lower down in my body. I bellowed then, and the cry was deep and huge, evidence of a power that seemed alien but must have come from me, a power I could channel but not command.

As my body opened, the pain was ecstatic—*ek-static*, in the sense of the Greek roots of the word—that is, I stood outside myself. My field of vision was shortened to arm's length and then dissolved. Borderless, I craved touch, needed skin on my skin and the pressure of hands and elbows to open me up and hold me together. There was a fissure, and for some time I occupied a liminal space between self and world. Hearing voices that exhorted it to bear, my body bore down. Cloudbreak, and return, and then a baby on my breast, looking up into my face.

There is not a lot unique to this story; it lines up pretty nicely with other accounts—from *The Girl* ("I felt all the river broke in me and poured and gave and opened"), from Friedrich's article ("something elemental and stupendous was happening and I was in on it") and from the slew of anecdotes included in Ina May Gaskin's classic *Guide to Childbirth*. In the aftermath, writes Friedrich, "you are no longer yourself alone, but a force; the memory stays with you and makes you strong and released." This is what can come of the experience of necessity as something other than trauma—a liberating intimacy with the immanent force of life.

•

"They made a little cave in the corner." This sense of enclosure, of invulnerability through the presence of intimates, goes a long way toward allowing life to come through over the objections of the self-conscious mind. Privacy is not essentially a question of the presence or absence of other people, as all of us who have been "in private" with others surely know. Rather, it is a feeling of being sheltered, of safety in vulnerability and permission to let go.

In my own case there was a happy coincidence of luck and privilege. I was in a room with people who made a cave around me. Sheltered therein, I had no reservation about being animal. This permission made me invulnerable, a feeling that I carried with me when I walked the halls in the hour before it all went down, to the horror of the new orderlies on the floor. (I half-heard a bored desk attendant offer assurance—"She didn't take the drugs.")

Could this necessary self-abandon have proceeded if I did not feel sheltered? The body has a sense of fear or safety, precognitive and wholly prior to our rationalizations. To feel vulnerable to the eyes of others, to their designs or interventions, is to want to maintain some semblance of control. The illusion of sovereignty that we cultivate in public is precious, not easily relinquished. The ambition to maintain it is antithetical to the necessary labor of childbirth. Apropos of nothing, my cousin, in her second trimester, told me her fantasy of hiding away to give birth "like an animal." It makes sense when you think about it: not wanting a hungry bear to eat the baby, not wanting to be seen so deep in suffering.

Lots of my friends now have had babies, and their birth stories run the gamut. Sometimes the body will not open up, and what follows is mundane (emergency C-sections are mundane in the U.S.) or grisly or tragic. Too often, the "bad labor" stories are the ones that also involve a callous doctor, a hostile nurse, a coldly clinical setting or lack of support—things that make a body feel afraid. The need for privacy, for a sense of being sheltered, of being secure and among intimates, has been largely ignored by mainstream obstetrics.

There are some practical fixes that would foster this sense of security in the clinical setting. First and foremost, there should be a way to dim the lights. This would seem like a no-brainer, but many hospitals have you under fluorescents through the whole ordeal. To the extent that it is practically possible, the room ought to be less clinical, the bed out of the direct sightline of the door. And for God's sake, there must be a way to block the view of the machine to which the laboring woman is tethered, which registers the time and intensity of each contraction along with a host of other statistics of vitality. Damned if that thing didn't make me *nervous*. Looking at it as the labor progressed, I became a number-crunching monitor of my uterine performance, unable to go with the flow of pain and release that coursed through me. Nothing really got started until my mother gently chastised me to turn my attention to the other side of the room. That these suggestions tend to be out of line with maximally efficient surveillance raises the question of whose prerogatives determine the experience.

•

Giving birth afforded me a fresh perspective on Arendt's distinction between what should be hidden and what should be shown. This binary of private and public remains deeply problematic regarding questions of domestic work and caregiving. But from another angle, privacy is not so much a question of what is *fit* for appearance to public eyes as of what cannot fully *transpire* in view of others. The idea that privacy is proper to the realm of necessity need not be based on shame in the body. Privacy can also shield interests that are literally vital, so as to give them their full weight.

As so often happens when one returns to a beloved book after a change in life, passages that I previously overlooked in *The Human Condition* now glow with significance. "The non-privative trait of the household realm," Arendt writes, "originally lay in its being the realm of birth and death which must be hidden from the public realm because it harbors the things hidden from human eyes and impenetrable to human knowledge." Her gestures to secrecy and mystery, hiddenness and sacredness, connote the potential amplitude and importance of the human relationship to the force of nature, of life. Some things should be hidden not because they are shameful, but out of respect for the sheer magnitude of their force. Arendt argues that only by knowing this force in its profound intensity can we really appreciate the kind of freedom we realize in the public world.

Ultimately, Arendt's distinction between private and public is both untenable and real. The plasticity of our experience and the demands of justice for the people who feed mouths and clean up shit preclude a neat distinction between what should stay hidden and what should appear. Even so, when the exigencies of life unbind the self, exposing sovereignty as the fiction it is, the human animal hides itself. There, in the dark, one is at liberty to suffer. Life becomes palpable as a force—and, at the extreme, so does the edge of death.

Arendt counted both romantic and charitable love among the phenomena that rightly belong to the private realm; she maintained that in full view of others, love and *caritas* become shallow and disappear. I will spare you the tired discourse on the Kardashianization of late modernity and only say that private matters have become public in new and previously unimaginable ways, ways that induce new forms of pleasure and power, which may come at the expense of other, older forms.

This new power and pleasure manifest the brightness and the shallowness, the virtuosity and ephemerality attendant to public life. For me, the sheltered abandon of a fully felt labor affirmed the potency of another pleasure, the delight of another power, no less potent or delightful for the fact that it hides.

Andrei Roiter, *Surveillance Camera*, 2007

PRIVATE LIVES

by Thomas Meaney

Technology has recently made surveillance by governments more effective than ever, but it was the Fascist and Communist states in the twentieth century that turned surveillance into high art. Chief among their innovations was to hand over the work to their own citizens. The Bolsheviks, and their heirs who came to power in postwar Europe, made a virtue out of mutual spying. In his *Memoir of a Revolutionary*, the ideologue-in-chief of the Yugoslav Communists, Milovan Djilas, justified the practice:

> Supervision of our private lives was essential if we were to have a new party and a dedicated membership. It didn't mean constant surveillance, but rather the right to supervise whenever the party's interests were threatened, interests for which we leaders stood and which we defended in the name of the entire membership.

The right to supervision! The right to surveillance! It sounds sinister now, but it went without saying at the time that the Communists could not have maintained the *esprit de corps* and internal organization necessary to defeat the forces of European fascism without it. For Djilas and his fellow partisans, surveillance was a necessary means for advancing the proletarian cause. They therefore made a habit of ideologically X-raying one another's interiors, much as the revivalists of the Great Awakening scrutinized each other's souls.

For liberal states, by contrast, spying was almost always a limited project—and, generally speaking, liberal regimes have not succeeded in convincing their citizens to report on one another. (Hoover was a better survivor than the NKVD's Lavrentiy Beria, but his rate of collection paled in comparison.) Even apparently innocuous data collection initiatives like the census have a complicated history. In 1939, Dorothea Lange could take a photo of an Oregonian lumberjack displaying the tattoo of his social security number on his bicep, proud to be collected and counted. Half a century later in the Federal Republic of Germany, crowds of thousands, still worried about a police state, protested the census and the collection of information as basic as their home addresses. Today the dominant mood is neither pride nor anger but apathy, whatever newspaper columnists would have us believe. Liberal societies have gathered quantities of data beyond the dreams of the most ambitious Communist bureaucrat—yet protests have been comparatively mild, and few have chosen to withdraw from the online portals where most of the spying gets done.

Mass indifference on the part of those who feel they have nothing to hide is only one major obstacle to liberal states rededicating themselves to the division between private and public spheres. Another is that, even among those who actively oppose the surveillance state, there exists little inclination to specify what privacy is actually good for. Indeed, privacy seems to have become such a naturalized sacred right in the liberal imaginary that it no longer seems necessary to make a new positive case on its behalf. Even some of the most vocal opponents of surveillance—Glenn Greenwald, Dave

Eggers, Rand Paul—have tended to reflect our confusion about the value we place on privacy in contemporary society, combined with a surprising lack of interest in how it came to be considered such an important value in the first place. Yet we need to know just what it is we love.

•

The root of the word is of little help: it derives from the Latin *privare*, to deprive. In the Roman Empire, honor fell to the *vir publicus*—the public man, someone honored for his service to Rome—not a *privatus*, a private individual, without any claim to status. The nullifying flavor of the term has mostly vanished in English, except in the military where the lowest rank is still "private." Originally, "private" designated that a solider was not a nobleman but a mercenary or a slave, who could be bought and sold.

Just as the Germanic tribes left the Roman public man in ruins, so their descendants during the Reformation emphasized private conscience and a personal relationship with God over the Church-mediated religion of papal Rome. But a more straightforward idea of privacy, also still familiar to us, was popularized as the result of the confrontation between Europeans and the peoples of the New World. When Bernal Díaz entered the city of Tenochtitlán in 1519, he made special note that the barbarians did outdoors what the Europeans did in private. It was partly out of the need to justify new global hierarchies that, by the eighteenth century, a proper understanding of "privacy" was seen as being a precondition for the distinguishing virtue of "civility."

It was not until the eighteenth century, however, that privacy began to take on the significance that it has for today's debates. For European elites following Rousseau, privacy was associated less with civility than with a new and more amorphous moral imperative, now known as *authenticity*. In his political philosophy, Rousseau imagined a society in which individuals could legitimately subsume their private interests, but he considered actually existing society to be a mostly corrupting influence on the individual. In his famous work on education, he prescribes his philosophical guinea pig, Emile, more than a decade of isolation in order to fully develop his capacities before entering into marriage and society. Yet in his *Confessions*—the first great modern tell-all—Rousseau also provided a model for how to "share" one's authentic private experiences with the public. The result was a surge of vapid diarists, all anxious to prove that they too had a singular inner life.

The Age of Authenticity was also the age of the modern novel—another genre for which Rousseau's contribution was transformative. His *Julie*, read by some as his most persuasive articulation of the ethics of authenticity, was the best-selling book of its century in Europe. French novelists of the next century were left with no choice but to reckon with it. One of Flaubert's great insights was to see that vapidity itself did not mean an absence of genuine feeling. When Madame Bovary's lover Rodolphe becomes bored by his mistress's clichéd outpourings, it is not her but him that Flaubert condemns: "He did not distinguish—this man of so much experience—the difference of feeling beneath the sameness of expression." It's a distinguishing mark of "modern" humans, in any case, that we feel the need to *prove* that

Andrei Roiter, *Big Brother*, 2009

our inner life is not hollow. Later novelists continued to play variations on the theme: Proust and Joyce could get away with writing about the minutiae of private life in part because of their mock-epic style, which carried their quotidian freight to philosophical destinations. A more radical risk has been taken by Knausgaard, who has forsaken the safeguard of style altogether: the Norwegian raises the stakes of authenticity by telling his story in the most artless sentences possible.

But what is the link between the cult of authenticity and the sort of privacy that works toward the social good in a liberal polity? From one perspective, the widespread retreat among artists and philosophers into the caverns of the self was a testament to the fading promise of Romantic politics; having failed to transform Europe in the wake of the Age of Revolution, they would have to rest content with transforming their inner selves instead.

At the same time, there was one slice of eighteenth-century society that did attempt to create a bridge between privacy as a self-oriented value and privacy as a precondition for the effective reform of society. This was the cult of Freemasonry. The Masonic associations were seedbeds for the revolutionary tumult that would eventually bring down the ancient regimes of Europe. Their lodges, shrouded in secrecy, were thought to allow space for the development of the moral authority they needed to question the state. A pamphlet from a German lodge in 1859 states that the private lodges do "what neither the state nor the church can. [They] will increase and spread inner virtue and probity." But they were also meant to protect those who wanted to think and organize against the prevailing politico-economic order without being crushed or infiltrated in advance.

The Freemasons shared with Rousseau the belief that society at large was tyrannical and judgmental; but although they advocated a temporary isolation, the aim of that isolation was ultimately not to transcend society but to improve it. The criterion for exemplary democratic citizenship among the Masons became the ability to leave the pressures and the eyes of society for a period, think through one's own interests as well as society's, and then return a more sovereign citizen, better able to contribute to the common good. The Masons saw themselves, like Rousseau, as undertaking nothing less than the construction of a new man, but this would be a person who did not define himself against politics. A moral citizen who possessed the required skills for bettering the commonweal through the democratic art of persuasion: this was their goal.

•

Today's liberals often conflate the self-fashioning privacy of Rousseau and the more publicly oriented privacy of the Masons—for instance, here is Glenn Greenwald, at the height of the debate over the NSA surveillance program:

> We all need places where we can go to explore without the judgmental eyes of other people being cast upon us. Only in a realm where we're not being watched can we really test the limits of who we want to be. It's really in the private realm where dissent, creativity and personal exploration lie.

On the one hand, Greenwald presents privacy as necessary for the internal development of the individual in the Rousseauean mode. On the other, he names it as a place for the development of "dissent" in the political sense that would have been more familiar to the Masons.

To tie together these two kinds of privacy can be productive; Pussy Riot was at least partly effective in passing off political critique as spontaneous art. But to think that dissent flows naturally from creative expression, or always overlaps with it, is to miss what is actually being threatened by developments such as the President's Surveillance Program. It is safe to assume, that is, that the NSA has little interest in suppressing our inner creativity—it may, on the other hand, believe it has good reasons for tracking our "dissent." This means it is most acutely in its *public-oriented* sense that our privacy is currently under attack—at least from the government. (Google and Facebook, which have more of an interest in aggregating and shaping tastes and desires, are another matter.)

One might argue that public-oriented privacy is already well ingrained in modern liberal thought and upheld in our laws. Indeed, one of the more durable insights of Millian liberalism is that it is in the long-term interest of an evolving polity for citizens to have a place to think beyond it unmolested. But the exception to the rule— the state's right to defend itself against those who wish to agitate violently against it—has always been vulnerable to exploitation. It is possible that many of the current social movements that require the most privacy to advance—the growing collection of student debt-strikers preparing coordinated actions on the internet, for instance, or the Chicago artist Leo Selvaggio's URME Surveillance project, which provides customers with 3-D masks of Selvaggio's face that can trick facial recognition cameras—will be infiltrated by the state before they fully enact their protests. When it comes to creating the kind of pressure on our public institutions that goes beyond words, it is this kind of privacy—the privacy which provides cover for groups to organize and plot different social futures— that is the most in need of defenders from the rest of the public, whether they agree with them or not.

Giorgio Barrera, *Finestra #37-2*, 2002
All images from the *Through the Window* series

BEING KNOWN

by Lowry Pressly

There comes a point in Krzysztof Kieslowski's 1994 film *Three Colors: Red* when the fashion model (that is, the professionally looked-at) Valentine (Irène Jacob) finds herself, after a series of fateful accidents, to be standing in the house of a retired judge and listening to a telephone conversation playing through some sort of stereo repurposed for surveillance. She stares into the glowing dials and hears a kind of argument: evidently, the two men on the phone are clandestine lovers engaged in the kind of humiliating pleading that such lovers have to suffer and inflict when circumstances conspire to keep them apart. When Valentine confronts the judge, he admits without shame that he is eavesdropping on the phone calls of his neighbors, nearly all of them, and that no one but himself, and now Valentine, knows. The judge taunts Valentine to inform the neighbor of his spying. She accepts his challenge, but when she arrives at the spied-upon man's house and sees his wife and, a moment later, his daughter—who is also listening in on her father's conversation—she thinks better of it. Valentine chastises the judge for violating the privacy of his neighbors—"It's disgusting," she says—but she chooses to keep it a secret to prevent the harm of breaking up the neighbor's family (or, if the daughter understands and tells what she hears, then to relieve herself of any guilt or blame connected with the dissolution). The film goes on and the eavesdropping eventually comes to light, but I want to stop it here, with this ambiguous moral resolution, in order to ask: Why, before they had been affected by the intrusion, was it a bad thing for the judge to violate the privacy of his neighbors?

A similar question came to mind recently when I heard Glenn Greenwald interviewed about the NSA's massive program of phone and email surveillance. After Greenwald described the many ways we have been surveilled without cause or warrant, his interlocutor posed what has become a very common question: he asked Greenwald if he had any hard evidence of harms suffered by individuals as a result of this program. Greenwald did his best to respond, but I wanted to blurt: *Of course there's evidence of harm; it's the evidence of the spying!* But my reaction raised the same question as the first act of Kieslowski's film, namely: Is there harm in being observed if I never find out about it and if my life is never affected in any observable way?

At first this might sound like a tree-falling-in-the-woods type of problem. One could fairly ask: If I never find out about the invasion of my privacy, how can it be said that I was harmed? Such a question is motivated by two important assumptions: one is the assumption that, barring some *Truman Show*-level conspiracy, it is safe to assume that if I never find out about the violation, then my life was not meaningfully affected by it; the other is that privacy is an instrumental good. According to the instrumental understanding of privacy, I want privacy because I want other things that would be impossible or at least more difficult to achieve without my privacy being respected. In other words, when you violate my privacy by monitoring my internet activity or by listening to my phone calls, you can interfere with my personal ends and projects. Violations of pri-

Giorgio Barrera, *Finestra #41*, 2007

vacy are harmful to me insofar as they stymie my goals, aspirations, etc.

Another way of expressing the instrumental view of the situation in my truncated version of *Red* is: "No harm, no foul." And it doesn't seem that the judge's neighbors, whom he has been monitoring for some time, have had their lives altered in the slightest by his listening in on their phone calls—the judge lives alone, has told no one about the surveillance and doesn't even record the conversations. But, like Valentine, we suspect that there is a wrong here and that it consists in the violation of the person's privacy. So there seems at once to be no harm—at least no instrumental harm—and an evident foul. How to square these conflicting intuitions? When I imagine feeling violated by having my privacy somehow invaded by an unseen snooper—that is, when I put myself in the shoes of one of the judge's targets—is there a real violation to which my feeling refers, or is it a kind of phantom pain? To put it another way, what kind of harm could there be in simply being known?

•

Imagine that a bored hacker halfway around the world is monitoring your computer activity for reasons she does not entirely understand. She sees every keystroke, every bad draft and every strange web search, though she never does anything with this information, and your life—your reputation, your personal and career prospects, your psychological well-being, etc.—is not affected in any observable way. Nor do any systemic harms follow, like the kind that have come from some state-sanctioned programs of surveillance. Clearly *your* privacy has been violated and, therefore, it seems that *you* have suffered harm. But what might this harm be?

If you discover that you have been betrayed by someone, you are hurt and angry not because the betrayal was brought to your attention, but *because you were betrayed*. Indeed, even in the case where you never discover that you have been double-crossed, it feels like the betrayer was nevertheless wrong to do what he did and that you, as the one betrayed, have still suffered harm. In just the same way it seems clear that even if you never find out that someone has been monitoring your internet traffic or watching you in the shower, you have still suffered a violation of your privacy. This means that the violation itself is the harm, not the feeling that follows from its discovery. A feeling of violation is surely also a bad thing—it is an unpleasant experience, to say the least—but if the harm of being known consisted entirely in the sense of violation, we would find ourselves trapped in a circle (i.e. you feel violated because you feel violated) and no closer to explaining how it could be bad for you to be observed by your secret hacker, or to understanding what privacy is for. From some general ethical perspective, it seems the hacker has acted wrongly toward you, but this judgment does not account for the fact that what she has done is bad *for* you. Yet this again invites the question: Bad how, or, bad in what way?

One way of resolving our conflicting intuitions of "foul and no harm" in this case might have something to do with the kind of thing a self is. By "self" I just mean what we generally mean by that word: the expansive answer to the questions "Who am I?" and "Who is Lowry Pressly?" given by me and others respectively. At some level we all know that who we are is not completely up to us; it's why we keep most of what we think to ourselves, and it's why we wear one face at work and another within the confines of our homes. The person I think I am is quite different from the person (or persons) the world thinks I am, and the gap between the two matters to me—which significance would be a kind of psychopathology if how others knew us had no effect on who we know ourselves to be.

So, what are the consequences of the social self for the experience of being known? To begin to answer this question, let's compare the self to a crow skull. The crow skull on my desk has certain intrinsic properties: it is the shade of white that crow skulls of a certain age tend to be, weighs about one-eighth of a pound, is pretty smooth to the touch, etc. It also has certain relational properties: it is my skull, it belonged previously to a living crow, I found it in a certain river and so forth. One day you are passing by my house and you stop to look through my window, you lay eyes on the skull and then you move along. Nothing about the skull, it would seem, has changed by the fact of your seeing it. One's self, however, is unlike a crow's skull in at least one very important way. What I call my self is in part constituted by the looks of others; their seeing and recognizing me (as a fellow human, as a writer, as a failure, etc.) matters for who I am. How I appear to the world of others is what gives me my objective existence, and it is through dialogue with and struggle against this objective self that I become who I am. Society not only gives me that objective existence, but also reflects it back to me as my self. Consider, for example, these lines from Yeats's "A Dialogue of Self and Soul":

How in the name of Heaven can he escape
That defiling and disfigured shape
The mirror of malicious eyes
Casts upon his eyes until at last
He thinks that shape must be his shape?

This is not a new thought, of course. Philosophers from Hegel to Adam Smith to Charles Taylor have recognized that who I am is not entirely up to me. So too Sartre—"When I am alone, I can not realize my 'being-seated'; at most it can be said that I simultaneously both am it and am not it. But in order for me to be what I am, it suffices merely that the Other look at me." So too Yeats, though in the lines quoted above the poet does better than these philosophers at evoking the sheer coercive force that one's social self can exert on one's personal conception of who one is. Jeremy Bentham once based a whole architecture of punishment on the tremendous psychological power wielded by the invisible omnipresence of even a possible gaze. One could also recall Adam Smith's falsely accused man, who will inevitably begin to think of himself in the terms used by his accusers, or why the phrase "if you only knew what everyone *really* thought of you..." can be so cruel. One of the reasons shame is such a powerful emotion is that we are made to feel that we are in fact, in our secluded subjective selves, the objective self that exists in the unreachable minds of others, defenselessly subject to their appraisals: we are what they make of us *and nothing more*.

So what does this have to do with the harm in being known? It may be admitted that our selves are constituted in large part by how we are seen and known by others and still objected that the situation in which you are being spied on by one individual affects you in this way not at all. Or all of this

Giorgio Barrera, *Finestra #25*, 2007

may be granted and one could still object that the harm is instrumental if it entails interference with the shaping and control of your public persona. Fair enough—yet these objections still miss the point by a hair. Suppose you have an abiding and yet shameful interest in, say, graffiti art, and accordingly you spend a great deal of time online researching the history of the form, its virtuosos and so forth. And suppose that across the world your solitary hacker is monitoring your every keystroke without your knowledge, and without ever sharing her findings with anyone. In this case, you will live your whole life without having your social self reflect this information that you did not want it to reflect. You can become a crusader against graffiti if you like, and you can be known and remembered as such by your friends, family and countrymen. The harm thus characterized—the one you do not suffer—would be instrumental in the sense that the violation of your privacy interferes with your project of projecting a certain self-image onto the world of others. So then what sort of non-instrumental harm could your self have suffered from this violation of your privacy?

If your internet searches concerning illicit wall painting (or your medical ailments, political affiliations, etc.) are not exposed, then there is always the possibility that you might become a person who does or does not love street art, or who does or does not have chronic pain or genital lesions (or who has never or always loved or had such things). Your self might never be *solidified* in this way—there might always be some indeterminacy or ambiguity regarding your tastes, health and turn-ons for the world of others, of course, but also for your own self-conception. Once your search history is known, however, it's no longer possible for you to be one thing or the other, both and neither, if only for this one antipodal hacker. Who you are, in a very real way, has become a little more concrete, and it is this person whom you will now potentially be forced to confront in the alienating mirror of society's eyes.

If the stranger monitoring your internet traffic sees you as someone interested in graffiti art, then there is no way you can ever be someone who wasn't interested in graffiti art, if only for this one person. You might actually have a bred-in-the-bone antipathy bordering on hatred for all pictures on walls, but now that the other knows you as an aficionado, either (a) in the case of the knower whose snooping you have become aware of, you are now forced to respond, further exposing yourself, or you can leave it; or (b) you do nothing, as in our case of the unknown knower when there literally is nothing you can do. By looking at you or by monitoring your internet traffic, the unknown knower robs you of some of the possibility that is inherent in your self as a social creature. And it makes about as much sense to say that she robs you of that possibility without your permission as it does to say that I stole your TV without your permission. In other words, it's not the transgression of the bounds of consent that is at issue here; rather, it is something deeper, something that more directly affects who we are. The multitudes that you contain, to paraphrase Whitman, have decreased in number as a result of your being known.

•

Giorgio Barrera, *Finestra #11a*, 2003

Being known is a problem for celebrities, of course, and for people whose image is their livelihood; accordingly, U.S. tort law has developed to protect the privacy of those selves that command a premium in the marketplace. But if the harm is not a harm to one's reputation or a hindrance of one's ends (even in the project of self-making), but rather consists in the solidifying or reifying of one's possibilities, then it seems that harm would pertain to your self as the object of a single, unknown knower, as well as to the movie star caught by paparazzi playing bongos in the buff. And if that's the harm, then the difference between one person and the whole world knowing you in this regard is one of degree and not of kind. It is probably worse for one thousand people to know you as the result of a privacy violation than it is for the single snooper in our example, but that does not mean that the latter case is not bad for you.

Whether this kind of harm disappears when the knower forgets or dies, I am not sure. In a strange way, being known calls to mind the extramission theory of vision, which supposed that being seen consisted in being literally touched by beams emitted from the seer's eyes. It is hard to imagine that the harms of a solidified self and of stolen possibilities mean much after the knower no longer knows. Perhaps the harm ought not to be looked at from an atemporal standpoint, then, but rather in terms of one's entire life. It does seem sensible to say that it was bad that you were deprived of some possibility for a time, even if you did eventually get it back (the same way it is still wrong for me to steal your TV even if I give it back after the Super Bowl).

Perhaps ultimately it might not make sense to insist on the strict separation of "being known" from the modifying phrase "without my permission." Maybe there is, in fact, something essentially permissory about being known. The experiences of willingly exposing ourselves to others through relationships of love, friendship, camaraderie and the like demonstrate to us the value of giving and receiving permission to know and be know. Because of this, when we think about privacy violations, we look first for failures of permission. Indeed, part of what makes the bonds of intimacy so strong is the willing solidification of one's self before the mirror of another's eyes. Even so, it still seems there might be something to our other intuition, that there can be harm in simply being known, that even if a gaze cannot literally touch us it can still shape us from afar.

THE SOCIAL FILTER

by Rob Horning

In May, Facebook made a widely reported change to its default privacy settings for the site's new users, setting the audience for posts to "friends"—those users have chosen to connect with—rather than "public," meaning anyone who uses the internet at all. It also announced plans to have a blue dinosaur pop up in a window and walk users through a "privacy checkup." At least Facebook has a sense of humor about having tried to make privacy extinct.

Back in January 2010, when Facebook made the opposite move, setting its defaults to public, CEO Mark Zuckerberg declared that "people have really gotten comfortable not only sharing more information and different kinds, but more openly and with more people ... We decided that these would be the social norms now and we just went for it." The company sounded a different note in "Making It Easier to Share With Who You Want," the post announcing its recent change: "We recognize that it is much worse for someone to accidentally share with everyone when they actually meant to share just with friends, compared with the reverse."

Such rhetoric suggests that online privacy is just a matter of deciding who can see what we put online—but the stakes extend far beyond our visibility. In the introduction to *The Offensive Internet*, a collection of essays about online privacy issues, editors Martha Nussbaum and Saul Levmore list four distinct ways to conceive of the stakes of privacy:

There is the value of *seclusion*, which is the right to be beyond the gaze of others. There is *intimacy*, in which one chooses with whom to share certain information and experiences. There is also the interest in *secrecy*, which is to information as seclusion is to the physical person. And then there is *autonomy*, which is the set of private choices each person makes.

Facebook has shown an increasing willingness to cooperate with users' demands for control over the first three of these, as "Making It Easier to Share With Who You Want" makes plain. But the company respects your wish for "seclusion," "intimacy" and "secrecy" only because it does not respect your autonomy. Its privacy controls encourage users to conceive of privacy as being mainly about one's visibility to other users—but this creates a smokescreen with respect to the more significant privacy threat: Facebook itself. Having established itself as a kind of all-purpose connective tissue in the social lives of over a billion people, the company is now using its monopoly position to exercise opaque control over the shape of social interaction, manipulating the flow of information in ways users don't understand and can't interrupt.

This became evident a month after its announcement concerning privacy, when journalists began to take notice of a paper on "emotional contagion" published by data scientists working with Facebook. This study revealed the company's eagerness to covertly shape the feelings of its users by playing with what shows up on their News Feed. To Facebook's apparent surprise, many users were outraged at its having made them subjects in a vast mood-manipulation experiment.

Caleb Hahne, *Distant*, 2014

But the experiment demonstrates concretely what has been true ever since Facebook introduced its black-box methods for managing users' News Feeds: privacy settings don't determine who sees what information; algorithms do—and these algorithms are optimized in Facebook's own interest.

That sort of intervention might not seem particularly problematic. After all, in its active management of what we see, Facebook is employing proven strategies from traditional commercial media, using ratings-like feedback (in the form of "likes" and other captured user behavior) to design programming that will hold viewers' attention and make it available to advertisers. Only Facebook is not an ordinary product. It's not something we consume more or less of based strictly on our individual preferences and our ability to afford it. It has become the platform on which many of us stage our social life. And if our friends are using Facebook, we have to use it to continue to belong. Not having a Facebook page can raise as many flags about one's reputation and conviviality as anything that might be discovered on the site; one simply cannot unilaterally disassociate from it without disqualifying oneself from a wide range of opportunities.

Unfortunately, this puts Facebook in a position to control which opportunities are revealed to whom. Now that its network is firmly entrenched, the company can work to impose the sort of social life it would prefer its users to have, using its control over what users see to influence whom they associate with and under what conditions. And the company is happy to auction that control off to whoever is willing to pay for it. Maybe a political party wants you to see only the updates of fellow party members, or only those that express doubt about opposing candidates. Maybe a car company wants you to see every update that mentions the pleasures of driving and none that complain of the drudgery of commuting. Can Facebook help? In principle, yes.

•

Perhaps we should think of Facebook users more as laborers for the company than as its clients. Unlike conventional entertainment companies, Facebook depends on its users to supply the raw materials (various instances of "sharing") to make its product (the News Feed calibrated for maximum "stickiness"). This requires a steady flow of what we might call "surplus sharing" from its workers, who are paid in the currency of attention from other workers, which Facebook's total control over News Feeds allows it to mint. Seen in this light, the company's attempts to address "privacy" show up as just one part of its strategy for managing its assembly line and mitigating workplace hazards that might slow production. From Facebook's perspective, privacy is a kind of transaction cost weighing on "peer productivity" within its vertically integrated social factory. Giving users apparent control over privacy settings pacifies their concerns and elicits more voluntary labor from them.

Yet Facebook treats its users not only as workers but also as products in themselves. The company collects data on its users in order to segment them into demographics that can be sold to advertisers. (Individuals may also purchase "reach," which increases the visibility of their posts, essentially turning them into ads.) When Facebook offers users more "control" over privacy settings, then, it

Caleb Hahne, *Loving You Has Become More Difficult*, 2014

is not only inducing them to perform more labor, but also collecting more data about their preferences, including which friends fit into which categories. Using the privacy controls serves Facebook's goal of better commodifying you.

Facebook purports to offer us the seemingly magical possibility of a social life that is at the same time more individualized and autonomous, a world in which we decide who and what appears by means of our decisions as to whom to befriend and which posts to like. In fact, Facebook structures the feed to suit advertisers' needs, putting users in spontaneous, provisional demographics to permit the perfect match between audiences and ad strategies. It can then track the effectiveness of those matches by correlating purchasing behavior with the many streams of data it compiles on users, including information about their activities outside Facebook's apps. As Derek Thompson of the *Atlantic* argues in describing Facebook's unique effectiveness as a phone-ad server,

> only Facebook combines (a) the simplicity of a single-column cascading product, (b) explicit information about who we are, what we like, and who we know, (c) controlled experiments that can connect online and offline identities to discover exactly how many people are seeing ads on Facebook and buying that product later, and (d) just ridiculous scale.

Facebook's desire to conduct these "controlled experiments" is why it refuses its users full access to how the site represents and structures their social lives—the sort of control the site seems to promise, particularly with its privacy settings. The sheer volume of content that Facebook serves to users and the opacity with which it serves that content render its manipulations subtle and unobtrusive.*

By keeping the mechanics of its algorithms private, Facebook refuses its users the autonomy its platform might otherwise seem to afford. Facebook defends its algorithmic processing as a way of filtering content for its users' benefit, based on their own revealed preferences. But without access to the algorithms, users have no choice but to take the company at its word on that. There is no way of knowing that Facebook is not experimenting with methods to reshape our preferences in accordance with advertisers' demands. (And indeed its mood-manipulation experiment makes that prospect seem highly likely, since it suggests that Facebook would calibrate its algorithms to display items that might intensify feelings of insecurity as long as that led to greater engagement with the site.) The same must be true for algorithmic filter bubbles that curtail users' sense of the breadth of opinion even within the social networks they themselves have built: if showing you only those updates that agree with your prejudices keeps you logged in and scrolling, that is what Facebook will do. Pushed to its logical conclusion, this would turn social interaction into a form of solitary consumption, augmented by the sort of Pavlovian reward schedules that gambling companies use to maximize players' time on gaming machines. It would transform

---

* According to a survey cited in "Uncovering Algorithms: Looking Inside the Facebook News Feed" by Christian Sandvig, Karrie G. Karahalios and Cedric Langbort, 62.5 percent of users were not even aware that their Facebook News Feed was filtered by algorithms; presumably they believe they can see everything their friends in the network want to share with them if they are willing to keep scrolling.

eagerness for communal participation into a mode of isolation.

•

The idea that individuals can use privacy settings or hack social networks to unilaterally secure their own personal security is a myth propagated by tech companies. It reflects a fantasy about how social life works, as an opt-in situation you can manage from a device with a variety of settings and filters. With its vast leverage over users' informational ecosystem, Facebook can shape the kinds of personal choices individuals make—not through a show of force or a threat of punishment, not by exposing their private information to others, but through its behind-the-scenes reshaping of what its users experience as real, as likely, as possible, as trending. By selling its information about users to third parties, data brokers, predictive-analytics companies and the like, it enables these firms to cross-reference the information, unearth behavioral patterns and correlations among large data sets, and use these findings to discriminate among (and potentially against) users invisibly. The ubiquitous networks crowding everyday life not only permit easy surveillance but also allow companies to inflect their treatment of customer segments without seeming to constitute a class that could sue them over it. With the help of Facebook and other Big Data companies, lenders, insurers and real-estate brokers can come up with de facto proxies for categories that they are officially forbidden from using in their decision-making processes.

Better control over the visibility of one's posts does nothing to address these kinds of threats and may actually make them worse. Users may feel it's safe to use Facebook more, to never shut it off, letting it passively accumulate more and more information, all of which remains putatively private. Yet this data allows social control to become highly individualized, as specific to us as we are expressive on social media. The more we share, the more finely attuned the control can be, to the point where it may simply seem like convenience: apps recommending what we should and should not read, who we should or should not listen to, where we should go and the route we should take, the food we should eat and the places we should sleep. The level of effort it would take to break out of these recommendation bubbles has become increasingly prohibitive.

Even if one waged a personal disinformation campaign against the data collectors, it would have little effect. From the perspective of the Big Data companies, such inaccuracies don't matter. They aren't interested in targeting specific individuals, just types—and the "privacy" harms they are responsible for are at the level of populations, not persons. As Woodrow Hartzog and Evan Selinger point out in their chapter on "Obscurity and Privacy" for the forthcoming *Routledge Companion to Philosophy of Technology*, "Even if one keeps a relatively obscure digital trail, third parties can develop models of your interests, beliefs, and behavior based upon perceived similarities with others who share common demographics." Regardless of what you have chosen to share, you can always be modeled more broadly. Companies like Facebook can ascribe simulated, probable data points to you, which will become factors in the way other institutions treat you, regardless of whether those probabilities are realities.

In a situation like this, conformity might be our best means of resistance. Instead of presenting a rich and complex personality on social media, the freest among us will offer only a contrived, superficial one.* Then we will have come full circle. Privacy that protects our intimate, revealing secrets will no longer matter, because we won't have anything truly personal to post.

---

* This was the ambition of "normcore," a fashion trend that championed the social camouflage of mundanity.

THE GENETIC SELF

by Nathaniel Comfort

Who hasn't thought of genetic engineering as a "brave new world"? In Aldous Huxley's eponymous 1932 novel, the One World State uses what we would now call in-vitro fertilization to create a genetically tailored, highly stratified society, kept complacent and happy with a drug called "soma." The book was a bitter, brilliant response to J. B. S. Haldane's sunny sci-fi story *Daedalus*, which first proposed the concept of IVF, or "ectogenesis." Haldane was a techno-optimist: he believed that science could address or even repair mankind's defects and weaknesses. Techno-pessimists such as Huxley, in contrast, take a darker view. For Huxley, the cultural authority of science inherently veered toward totalitarianism. Whether one is an optimist or pessimist, genetics is certainly changing our social roles, our social mobility, our social relations. Modern biology challenges conventional understandings of autonomy, surveillance and privacy. In short, advances in DNA science have surely placed us in some kind of brave new world—the question is, *which* kind.

WELCOME TO YOU

For a hundred dollars you can spit in a test tube, mail it off, and in a few weeks receive a detailed profile of your genes. "Welcome to you," proclaims the cheerful kit that arrives from 23andMe, a direct-to-consumer, or DTC, genomics company. The message on that box is unambiguous: your genes are your essential, true identity. If we accept that message, we permit a private company to deliver to us our selves. If we reject it, we alienate ourselves from a thriving genetic community that sees itself as the bright future: open, progressive, and winning the timeless war against illness, senescence and death. At first blush, the choice seems easy.

The notion that your genes are your essential self—genetic essentialism—is fairly recent. Although the idea that heredity contributes to our health and identity is ancient, the idea that for practical purposes it is all that matters dates only to the nineteenth century. The English statistician Francis Galton conceived of heredity as a subterranean stream of "germ plasm," flowing down the generations, isolated and insulated from the environment's buffeting of any individual body. In determining who we are, Galton wrote, nature was "far more important than nurture."

That stream was increasingly polluted, Galton was convinced. Vexed by the fact that people paid more attention to breeding their cattle than themselves, in 1883 he proposed a scheme of hereditary improvement he called "eugenics," meaning "well-born." The stream of British germ plasm could be socially filtered, and even enriched, by persuading the "fittest" people (borrowing loosely from Darwin) to have more children; the "unfit," fewer. A techno-optimist to the core, Galton believed that, given proper instruction, people would see the logic of this scheme and participate voluntarily. In this he was naïve—at least about the abstinence part. After 1900, eugenics became coercive, while the state's trust in the population shriveled. Marriage restriction and sexual sterilization

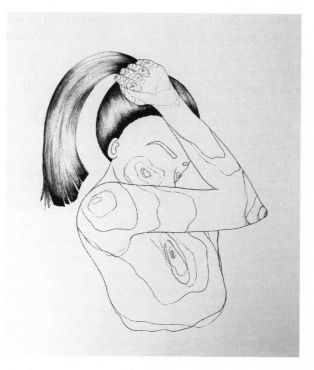

Flory Huang, *Untitled, no. 7*, 2014
From the *Sensus et intellectus ducta* series

laws were keystones of state-run programs of hereditary improvement. When most people think of eugenics, they think of a scientifically rationalized program of racial purification, which it was. But eugenics always had a medical and public health dimension as well. The vast majority of forced sterilizations were carried out in a medical milieu—particularly in psychiatric hospitals. Eugenic sterilization was considered preventive medicine for incurable mental or other hereditary disease. This is the origin of medical genetics. Mainstream genetic medicine today isn't eugenics, but it has a deep taproot in ideas of hereditary social control.

These medical roots of genetic selfhood shaped emerging notions of genetic privacy. When genetic tests for disease were introduced, beginning with phenylketonuria in 1960, their results were subject to the standards of medical confidentiality—and the shadow of eugenics hung over them. In the 1990s, for example, scandal erupted at the Lawrence Berkeley Laboratory in California, when it came out that prospective employees had been compelled to undergo tests for pregnancy, syphilis and sickle cell disease. (Sickle cell, a simple recessive genetic disease, was considered a "black" disease because of its prevalence in African Americans.) Positive tests for any of these conditions were grounds for rejection. The Ninth Circuit Court surely had no idea of the debt it owed to Galton when it ruled this policy unconstitutional, writing in the decision, "One can think of few subject areas more personal and more likely to implicate privacy interests than that of one's health or genetic make-up."

Like all medical records, genetic data has implications for employment and insurance. Yet genetics has always been treated as a special case. In 2008, after a dozen years of negotiation and revision, the Genetic Information Nondiscrimination Act (GINA) was signed into law. Past abuses, the authors reasoned, made genetic information particularly important to safeguard. As the law's name implies, its principal concern is discrimination on the basis of the ultimate pre-existing condition: your genes. Genetic test results thus joined other supposedly innate qualities, such as race, creed and gender, as characteristics for which it was illegal to deny someone a job, home or insurance policy.

Yet science always seems to race ahead of culture and bioethics, and therein lies a tension. Ironically, the more central genes become to science, the less central they become to biology. By that I mean that the more we study DNA, the more Galton's notion of an isolated, protected germ line seems to melt away. The genome proves to be highly dynamic, with gene activity and even gene structure changing over the course of a life. Further, our genome isn't ours alone: studies of the "microbiome" show that the genes one inherits are supplemented by those of the dozens, perhaps hundreds, of different kinds of microbes that live in our bodies. To cap it all, "genetic" no longer necessarily means "innate." Techniques such as gene therapy and genome editing enable us to imagine a future, perhaps not far off, in which we will modify our own genomes or those of our children. The more we learn, the more difficult it becomes to formulate a strict genetic definition of "me."

The evidence from the labs, then, strongly refutes genetic essentialism. Yet the idea not only persists—it has been strengthening. Recent news stories have covered the "gay gene," the "violent drunk" gene, the "couch potato" gene and even the "slut" gene. Not coincidentally, such headline-grabbing genes just happen to reflect contemporary social preoccupations. Dig deeper and it often turns out that the putative gene explains little: it may contribute only 2 or 3 percent of the risk for the condition; frequently it isn't a gene at all but merely a "marker," perhaps a single DNA building block, that correlates with the "trait."

The ever-widening gap between science's understanding of genetics and the public's understanding of science greatly complicates the idea of genetic privacy. For what exactly do I protect when I protect my genetic information? Is it "really" me—or only an idea of me? If an idea, *whose* idea? Almost paradoxically, the better we understand genomes, the more genetic identity becomes a social construct rather than a scientific fact. In contrast to humanistic methods of self-understanding, knowing our genetic identity requires interpreters. That 23andMe profile, after all, is not raw data but an analysis prepared by a company. The more biologists learn about genes, then, the more important it becomes to question who is constructing genetic identity. *Cui bono* here, anyway?

SEQUENCE JUST WANTS TO BE FREE

The explosive advances in genome sequencing in recent years have provoked a remarkable rethinking of medical privacy. A twist of the helix came just a year after the completion of the Human Genome Project in 2004. The genome project gave us a reference sequence for human heredity, but of course what's medically interesting is the ways in which we are different, not the same. In 2005, the Harvard professor George Church launched the Personal Genome Project (PGP). He

and nine other scientists, tech leaders, and a journalist agreed to sequence their genomes and put all the data on the web. The "PGP-10" branded themselves as brave pioneers in a new age of shared information. In the next three years, Craig Venter, the genome scientist, and James Watson, co-discoverer of the double helix, sequenced their own genomes and published them online. These celebrity sequences gave a burgeoning open-genomes movement valuable publicity.

Church and his followers promote genetic openness with evangelistic fervor. The PGP-10 added more members, and soon morphed into the 1000 Genomes Project. At the time of writing, a thousand had grown to 2,535. The group is still not much more than a sect, but because the members are highly educated and scientifically literate their potency exceeds their numbers. Prospective members are examined on their knowledge of genome science and privacy issues. They are the tech aristocracy. They won't be for long, however, if they meet their goals: their current target is to expand the congregation to 100,000 genomes.

Before deciding whether the gazillion genomes project is right for you, consider the following. Whether or not I believe my genome is "me," there is little doubt that it contains intimate, perhaps compromising information about me. (Watson, by the way, has since taken down his genome sequence.) Why should I share it with the world? *Don't think of yourself*, answer the PGPers. *Do it for the sake of medical research. Feed the database for the sake of the database.* Now, "medical research" is a complex beast. It is, among other things, a communal knowledge base ("scientific knowledge"); a body—thousands strong—of devoted, skillful, underpaid post-docs; an international, collegial and highly

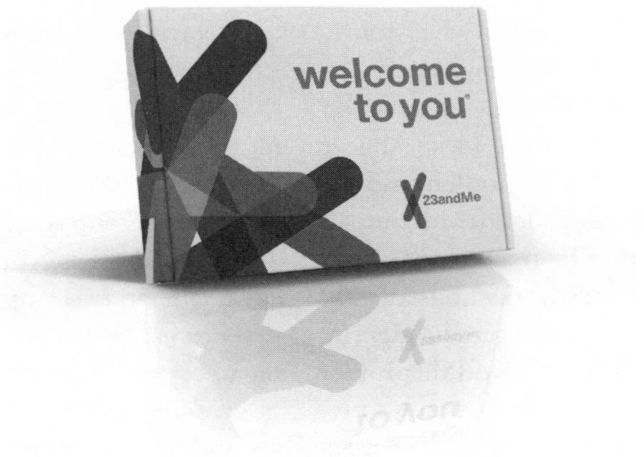
welcome
to you
23andMe

23andMe collection kit

competitive community of principal investigators; a legion of highly profitable nonprofit universities and medical schools; and a large for-profit sector that includes gratuitously wealthy biotech and pharmaceutical executives. The PGPers idealize medical research, neglecting its more mercenary elements. In the long term, of course, individuals (or, more likely, their children) may benefit from accelerated medical research: the hope is for improved diagnoses and therapies. But in the short term—where Americans think best—the impetus is not always so noble.

You needn't be a tech aristocrat to join a genetic community, however. Once you pay your C-note, spit in the tube and create an account with 23andMe or one of the other DTC genomics companies, you can join a variety of forums devoted to people who share some part of your genotype. Until recently, 23andMe offered both a genealogical and a health profile. In November 2013, the Food and Drug Administration shut down the health profile side on the grounds that 23andMe had repeatedly misled customers about the certainty of their genetic data. Many of those customers were outraged at the shutdown, however, and the company has since begun inching back into providing health information.

All genetic communities—whether they comprise tech aristocrats or what we might call the genetic proletariat—tend to have a populist bent. They think of genetic information as something that should not be the exclusive province of elite medicine. They are right about this. If you can interpret it accurately, having your genetic profile can provide communal support, and it may prompt proper medical consultation, positive lifestyle changes, further diagnostics, even prophylactic treatment.

However, it should be noted that these communities are often run by for-profit companies that collect and store your genetic information, largely without oversight. Data brokers, who buy and sell information about all of us, value health information above any other kind of data. A study by the investigative journalist Emily Steel showed that while demographic information such as age, gender and location was worth only $0.00005 per person, health information, such as specific diseases or drug prescriptions a person was taking was worth $0.26—5,000 times more. You think you get too many Viagra ads now? Imagine your inbox when your 23andMe profile suggests you have a 20-percent higher-than-normal risk of erectile dysfunction.

In sum, there is a tension between the rhetoric of the open-genomes movement and the funding, the knowledge base and the *sub rosa* statements of its leaders about why we should join up. It's worth asking how free that data is once we release it. Who is most likely to benefit—and what laymen can do to claim their share of the riches?

SCIENCE SAYS SO

DNA, of course, is only one half of the information revolution of the last half-century. Genetic information may remain the gold standard for identifying you as a person, but we now have electronic identities and communities as well. 23andMe offers a sense of certainty when it welcomes you to You. This certainty is largely illusory—it relies on a conflation of the fundamental with the unavoidable—but nevertheless, on the cultural level, genetic identity is stabilizing.

Electronic identities, on the other hand, offer fluidity. On the internet, avatars, screen names and other digital personas enable us to reinvent ourselves and form new kinds of communities without regard for geography, employment or other "true" identity.

The genetic and the electronic worlds are complementary in more ways than one. The four-letter code of DNA translates easily into computer binary. Your entire genome could fit on a CD. A highly detailed and annotated genetic profile could easily be copied onto a flash drive the size of your fingernail (and perhaps tattooed conveniently on your wrist or slipped, on a chip, subdermally). Conversely, DNA can literally store text. George Church at Harvard Medical School and Ewan Birney of the European Bioinformatics Institute have each developed DNA-based repositories that can store hundreds of times the contents of the Library of Congress in a droplet of DNA. Meanwhile, synthetic biologists such as Craig Venter treat the genome as a computer program. They are well on their way to "booting up" a completely artificial cell. Computing and genomics are rapidly merging into a single family of information industries—some dry, some wet. So intimate is this relationship that Anne Wojcicki, 23andMe's CEO, married Google cofounder Sergey Brin (although apparently the couple has since denatured).

Whether or not the creation of a gigantic commercial biosocial database was ever dinner-table conversation in the Wojcicki-Brin household, it is certainly happening. In 2013, the biologist Yaniv Erlich performed a creepy proof-of-concept experiment. Starting with (anonymized) DNA sequences from the 1000 Genomes Project, Erlich produced DNA profiles of individuals, searched public databases, made a few educated guesses and identified their names. From there, it was just a few clicks to find their Facebook pages, from which, of course, one has access to details of their sexuality, shopping preferences and "major life events" (marriage, pregnancy, jobs, etc.). And Facebook being what it is, one person's page links to those of family and friends. So by sharing your data you are also sharing others' data, nonconsensually.

These biosocial networks do have a genuine upside. In a recent *New Yorker* article, Seth Mnookin profiled Matt Might, a computer scientist at the University of Utah and a savvy blogger with a large internet following. When Might's firstborn son Bertrand showed signs of a mysterious disease, the family found a doctor who ordered the complete sequencing of Bertrand's exome (the 2-percent portion of the genome that codes for proteins). He found a mutation in a little-known gene called NGLY1; Bertrand apparently had an undescribed genetic disease. Might used his internet clout to find other cases. He wrote a blog post that went viral and, as it circulated, prompted other families with children with similar conditions to contact him and his team. There is still no treatment, but the initial research and community-building are underway.

Such stories are often used to illustrate the "democratization" of biology. High-tech biology, the narrative goes, is breaking out of elite academic labs and going public. So-called DIY biology is a growing movement of people who carry out genetic analysis and engineering experiments in their kitchens or in public or private "hacklabs." The slogan of Drew Endy's BioBricks Foundation, a leading exchange for biotech "parts" and "devices," is to pursue "genetic engineering in a responsible, ethical manner." The poster for DIYbio, the leading group promoting do-

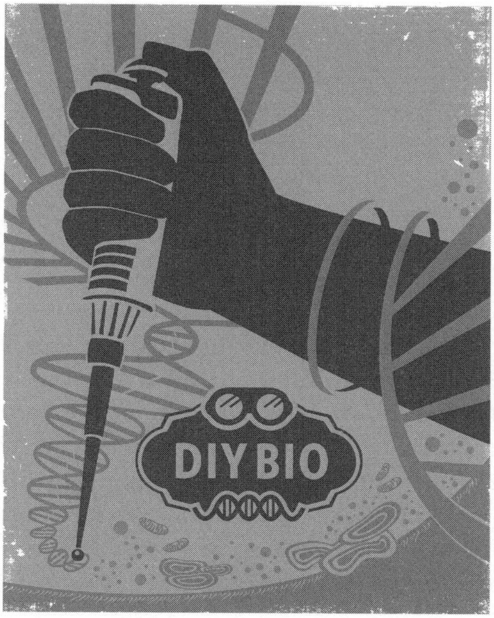
DIY BIO

DIYbio poster, 2008

it-yourself biotechnology, is a hand wrapped in a raised fist around a pipetteman, the molecular biologist's signature tool.

But this notion of genetic populism is romantic, if not disingenuous. According to one recent survey, more than a quarter of these amateurs already do research in an academic or corporate laboratory, and nearly one in five has a Ph.D. DIYbio may promise access to biotechnology for all, but practically speaking it is only available to those with the resources and training to use it. Indeed, achieving the democratic ideal of open access to genetic information will be far from straightforward. The techno-optimists seem to assume that once the technological problems are solved, the rest will follow automatically and without incident. In fact, developing the technology is the easy part. Historically, technology has not been a great friend of the working class, and heredity has been a potent tool for shoring up, not smashing, social boundaries.

"Big question is how to mainstream the process so don't have to be a @mattmight or connected to reap benefits of NGS [Next Generation Sequencing]," Mnookin wrote to me in a tweet. Big question indeed. Until we answer that one, the ability to sequence and understand genetic information will tend to be socially stratifying, not leveling.

COMMUNITY, IDENTITY, STABILITY

The motto of Huxley's One World State was "Community, Identity, Stability." We have seen that genetic information contributes powerfully to all three of these values. Genetic essentialism—the idea that our genes carry our fundamental essence—creates an almost irresistible sense of biological identity that seems independent of the state of genetic knowledge. Genetics contributes to the growing trend toward what the sociologist Nikolas Rose calls "biological citizenship"—communities based on health status, rather than on traditional qualities such as labor or nationality. And genetic information might well help stabilize and solidify social strata.

Those parallels do not place us in Huxley's dystopia. Our brave new world, it turns out, is not an authoritarian government but a strange new marketplace, in which privacy and identity are commodities. From Facebook pop-ups to grocery store discount cards, we constantly exchange our personal information for product suggestions or lower prices. By getting on the data grid, we turn our personal information into a commodity. In the brave new information society, retail companies seek to ease their products into your jeans (and sometimes your genes into their products) as easily and painlessly as possible. Today's "soma" is convenience.

Biology is an increasing part of this consumer culture. The new iPhone and Android phones can monitor and aggregate your vital signs, such as heart rate and blood pressure. Apps that provide this information could have real health benefits, such as alerting users to danger signs or motivating them to stick with their fitness regimens. But it's an illusion that your phone tells you this information. In fact, you tell your phone, which in turn tells the companies whose handy little apps you downloaded. Siri may ask, "Low energy? There's a Starbucks on the next corner. Shall I order your usual double skim latté and blueberry muffin? They will be ready when you get there." Perhaps iPhone 9 will measure serotonin levels. Maybe on iPhone 11 Siri will know your genome. "Given your tendency toward congestive heart failure, I've canceled your cable subscription, signed you up for a six-week aerobics class on Thursday nights, and switched your pizza order to a salad."

When we relinquish privacy and commodify our data, we should expect something in return. But doing the cost-benefit analysis with our genetic information is as tricky as it is important. We can be confident of two things, however. First, its exchange value is overrated. The persistence of genetic essentialism creates a bubble that consistently inflates the perceived value of genetic information. It is a seller's market. Second,

however, its use-value—what can actually be done with my DNA—is both unknown and in constant flux. Genetics *does* matter to health, of course, but in what ways and to what extent changes at the hectic pace of scientific discovery. For these reasons, it seems wise to share our genetic information judiciously and with due skepticism.

This brave new world need only be dystopian if we surrender our agency. If we are aware of the exchanges we are making and how our information is valued—if we are alert to the commodification of personal data—we can remain active players instead of becoming pawns.

reviews

Desdemone Bardin, *IAM Fête de l'Humanité*, 1991
All images originally published in the book *Freestyle* (1993)
Courtesy of Sebastian Bardin-Greenberg

BACK IN THE DAY

by Jesse McCarthy

IN 1988 NO one in France took the hip-hop movement seriously. It was the rec-room era. JoeyStarr and Kool Shen were just two kids from Seine-Saint-Denis, the 93rd ward, a neglected tract of housing projects on the northern outskirts of Paris. One black, the other white, they shared a love and talent for breakdancing and got together practicing moves in bleak lots and house parties. They started crews and listened to Doug E. Fresh, Masta Ace, Grandmaster Flash and Marley Marl. DJs played the breaks looped over jazzy horn riffs, cats sported Kangol hats and Cosby sweaters, and they tagged the walls of the city with their calling card: NTM, an acronym for *Nique Ta Mère* (Fuck Your Mother). There were no labels, no official concerts or shows, and the only airplay was after midnight on Radio Nova, a station dedicated to underground and avant-garde music, created and directed by French countercultural hero Jean-François Bizot.

I was at a house party in a spacious bourgeois apartment somewhere in the 16th arrondissement when I first heard DJ Cut Killer's track "La Haine," better known by its infamous refrain "*Nique la police*" (Fuck the police). I hadn't yet seen the film *La Haine* (1995), which made the song famous, and which remains arguably the most important French film of the 1990s. I was at a *boum*, slang for a teenage house party and a tradition of Parisian coming of age that involves a great deal of slow dancing and emotional espionage. Sophie Marceau immortalized it as a mesmerizing ingénue in the greatest French teen romance ever produced, *La Boum* (1980). But I wasn't dancing with Sophie Marceau. I was dancing with Caroline. A young dude interrupted Ace of Base and popped in a cassette he had brought in his jacket pocket. The party came to a jarring halt as everyone looked at everyone else trying to figure out what to do. The shock of hearing someone actually say "fuck the police" and repeat it again and again stunned me. The owner of the tape was bragging about how he got it. How it was banned, and you could only find it "underground." This turned out to be true, though I didn't believe it at the time. Caroline insisted she was impressed, but her body was limp, her eyes vacant. The song made a big impression on me. Even without fully understanding everything on the record, the exhilaration of open rebellion was palpable. Over an onslaught of breaks and scratches a voice shouted: "Who protects our rights? / *Fuck* the justice system / The last judge

I saw was as bad as the dealer on my corner / *Fuck the police / Fuck the police!*" KRS-One samples collided with a looping of Édith Piaf's "Non, je ne regrette rien." We understood the symbolism perfectly. The difference between Sophie Marceau's world and ours was the existence of the ghetto as an undeniable fact. The party was over.

I ARRIVED IN FRANCE in 1992, the year the Maastricht Treaty creating the European Union was signed and Disneyland opened its first European theme park outside Paris. I was still a kid and spoke not a word of French. It was not going to be easy figuring out how to grow up as a black American in Paris. The skin game was complicated. I was too light-skinned to be from Senegal, but dark enough to be from Algeria or Morocco. Declaring my Americanness, I soon learned, was necessary for avoiding a certain nastiness of tone specially reserved for the postcolonial subject. On the other hand, as an expatriate American at an international school, I was moving in bourgeois circles. Money cushions social realities and creates a haze of similarity among peers until you get to around sixteen, the age in Paris when you start to roam the city alone, have your first real crush, and learn how to roll a cigarette while waiting for the Métro.

The peripheral zone known as the *cités* or *banlieues* was terra incognita to me at that point. Nobody I knew had ever been that far off the map. You glimpsed the banlieue from the train, on your way to the countryside or the airport; its inhabitants lived there, trapped beyond the city walls, as though feudal relations had never really collapsed in the capital of the Revolution. I did know the symbol for that space: HLM, an acronym signifying a set of social-housing block towers grouped in pods of dreary urban sprawl. They were built during the years of the post-World War II economic boom the French call *les Trente Glorieuses*, when ex-colonial immigrants were imported into the republic as cheap labor for a country still rebuilding from the catastrophe of 1939-1945. The HLMs were exalted for their modern incarnation of Le Corbusier's ideal of sleek "towers in a park" and satirized for their sterile futurism by Jacques Tati in his classic film *Playtime* (1967). France has always had a rather anxious, and occasionally schizophrenic, attitude towards modernization.

But the architects of the utopian HLM did not account for the social and political effects of racial and historical prejudice. By the 1980s the boom had petered out, and the cheerful attitude towards cheap immigrant labor soured into an austerity-driven desire to push the immigrants and their children—born with French citizenship—back out. If not out of the country altogether, then out to the social housing blocks on the fringe of the cities—out of sight.

Resistance began in language. The French state has an obsessive attachment to the purity of the tongue. It maintains an academy devoted to policing grammar and ratifying vocabulary. In the early 2000s they declared that email would henceforth be called *courriel*, a derivative of *courrier* (mail). To this day all government employees have to send *courriel*. The rest of the country sends *mail*. Against this stodginess, the banlieue gelled around an outsider culture and generated its own idiom. "Verlan" is a play of word-flipping, where the first and last syllables of a word in French are inverted (*femme* becomes *meuf*, *l'envers* becomes *verlan*, etc.) By importing words from American English, and most of all Arabic words from across the Maghreb, the outsiders created their own counter-French, the creole of the ghettoized.

And yet, at least in the world of music, it seemed the newcomers would have to bend to the rules of French culture rather than the other way around. That strategy produced the first crossover hip-hop star, MC Solaar. It was Solaar who single-handedly established the literary imperative in French rap on his first album, *Qui Sème le Vent Récolte le Tempo* (1991). Solaar made a point of demonstrating his fluency beyond the street, taking on a hybrid troubadour-griot persona that situated him just within the orbit of *chanson française*, provocatively making himself heir to the likes of Jacques Brel, Georges Brassens and Serge Gainsbourg. In one of his singles he raps, "*L'allégorie des Madeleines file, à la vitesse de Prost*"—combining an allusion to Proust's madeleine with a nod to Alain Prost, France's Formula One racing hero of the Nineties. The near pun is not accidental.

Qui Sème le Vent was one of the first CDs I ever bought. The first couple of songs, heavily Gang Starr-influenced, were snappy enough. The second half of the album was less appealing, a half-baked dub collage. But smack in the middle was the track that would make Solaar instantly famous, a love ballad called "Caroline." I listened to that song over and over again. It was cheesy and sentimental and yet undeniably a feat of lyrical virtuosity. It evoked everything you could feel about first crushes all at once. The whole album still sounds in its very grain "old school," a term that has come to hover as a halo over a golden age of hip-hop bathed in what from our current standpoint looks like a shocking and enviable innocence. But there really is a greenness in Solaar's soft-spoken, almost-whispered delivery that connects with the green of Parisian sidewalk benches, where first cigarettes and first kisses imprint their weightless marks of identity. Solaar had the perfect pitch at the perfect moment: the overwrought saxophone riffs, the fanciful turns of phrase, the dub connection,

Desdemone Bardin, MC *Solaar*, 1992

the long Proustian sentences carrying over sixteen bars in a song. But it was for these same reasons that his artistry became instantly outdated, an artifact of nostalgia, something that could not keep in step with the cultural supercollider that hip-hop was forcing down the line.

F ILA SNEAKERS, LACOSTE caps, Sergio Tacchini tracksuits, one sock rolled up, a fur-lined bomber jacket, shaved heads, fanny packs for holding sticks of hashish the size and color of a caramel bar wrapped in tinfoil, tricked-out Yamaha scooters. By the mid-Nineties the profile had been established and the term *racaille* had entered the popular lexicon to describe a disaffected young man from the banlieues. Their arrival within the city walls was turbulent and disturbing. For the first time I was faced with a definitive "other." We knew that they didn't belong in our world any more than we belonged in theirs. There was no question of integration. And so it always seemed, at least to me, that everything was contested in the only public spaces we shared—in the public transportation system. I can never entirely dissociate racailles from the RER commuter trains with their acrid, low-grade plastic smell, the pallid lighting of underground transfer halls, the whine of the electric motors, and the fear of police patrols with German shepherds. There were acts of violence, some symbolic and others very real. You readied yourself for tense showdowns on empty platforms, you dreaded menacing whistles directed at your presence, and you practiced running up flights of stairs to the street. Entire areas in central Paris—Les Halles, Beaugrenelle and even the Champs-Élysées—became off-limits, even in broad daylight. Of course there was a complicating factor, namely that you also sought the same guys out to buy hash and weed. Dealers dropped by the high school on scooters to take numbers and chat about video games. But sometimes they were the same ones who got a crew together and jumped you for your wallet or your cell phone.

For most people, even in France, the idea of Paris is still heavily indebted to figments of a romantic Belle-Époque strain, whether colored like a Toulouse-Lautrec dorm-room poster, lifted from a black and white photograph of May '68, or raised to an arch postcard fantasia, as in Woody Allen's *Midnight in Paris*. *Frenchness* in this sense seems incompatible with hip-hop; even the language itself seems somehow unfit for rapping. To put it bluntly, this vision of Paris does not include immigrants of color. Despite my being on the bourgeois side of the class line, the Paris of color, of difference, could never be invisible to me.

It troubled me, made claims on me that I couldn't fully understand. Perhaps it bridged my own invisible loneliness. But it wasn't just me, or people like me. In our generation you had a choice: it was Suprême NTM or Daft Punk. And the choice felt deeply existential. Certain people would never be friends because of it. Plenty of kids chose to tune out the world and immerse themselves in the pill-popping scene of techno, house and electronica. Caroline was one of them. We never openly admitted why we grew apart. But it was there all the same. She wanted to go clubbing at the Rex on Saturdays; I tried ecstasy and decided it wasn't for me. From there it was two roads peeling away forever.

The club kids looked to London. If you were hip-hop, you turned to the USA. The most powerful impulse came from the West Coast, as Dr. Dre and the G-Funk era made their way across the Atlantic. Groups like Reciprok and Mellowman suddenly had the sounds of summer, and for the first time in its history, France had summer jams that weren't cheesy pop tunes à la Claude François. Tracks like "Libre comme l'air" (featuring a guest appearance from Da Luniz), "Balance-toi" and Mellowman's "La voie du mellow" were saturated with warm P-Funk chords usually heard whining out of low-rider trunks in Inglewood and Oakland.

In Paris the king of this sound was Bruno Beausir, a.k.a. Doc Gynéco. More than any other French rapper, Gynéco incarnated the ideal of adolescence. Laid-back, good-looking, smart, fresh gear, the guy who gets all the girls, has the best comebacks, has the best weed and wears the latest sneakers. He made having as your primary interests sex and getting high look really good. He sported a tight just-got-back-from-the-French-Open look: clean designer polo shirts, headbands under his natty dreads. On the cover of his album he slouches under a big Afro, showing off creased slacks and all white Adidas classics. He took the game up a notch. His rhymes were funnier, his references broader but also more popular: soccer, politicians, soap-opera starlets—in other words, television. His biggest hit, "Nirvana," is a quintessentially adolescent expression of ennui. "The hottest girls / You can have them / I'm tired of all that," he complains. "Tired of the cops / Tired of the gangs / Tired of life." In the refrain he gives a dopey lament about how he'd rather shoot himself in the head like Pierre Bérégovoy, François Mitterrand's prime minister, or go out fast like Ayrton Senna. When you're seventeen it doesn't get any better than that.

JUST AS HIP-HOP in the United States was concentrated for a time around East vs. West Coasts, the hip-hop scene in France quickly became oriented around two distinct and rival poles: Paris and Marseille. In Paris the three letters that mattered were NTM. In Marseille they were IAM. The latter were latecomers, but on their seminal album *L'Ecole du Micro d'Argent* (1997) the Invaders Arriving from Mars (short for Marseille) blew up instantly. IAM's rappers styled themselves after the Wu-Tang Clan and their tracks reflected a close study of RZA's production. In the mid-Nineties there was even a glimmer of hope for a transatlantic hip-hop empire, as rappers from New York collaborated with their French counterparts, with fascinating if somewhat mixed results. Like Wu-Tang, IAM presented themselves as a warrior horde. They took the names of Egyptian kings and kung-fu masters: Akhenaton, Shurik'n, Kheops, Imhotep. For a listener from Paris there was also the peculiar flavor of the southern accent, with its long vowels, and the insistence on the importance of Islam and political solidarity. But the rappers of IAM transcended geography and race; unlike their American counterparts, their case was built on a deeply entrenched class consciousness.

In the *quartiers nord* of Marseille the race line is blurry at best. Its residents are African, Arab, Creole, but also southern Europeans, particularly Portuguese, Corsicans and Italians, of which Akhenaton (Philippe Fragione) is a descendant. And most of the hip-hop generation comes from families that are likely to be mixed. In a port city like Marseille, though, the neoliberal factor is more readily evident than anything racial. What matters is inequality. The costs of the shadow economy are high, and the violence that comes with trafficking and corruption is unavoidable. In songs like IAM's "Nés sous la même étoile," drug money and the nihilistic culture it fosters are denounced for destroying youth, equality and promise: "Why was he always given after-school programs / Always vacation and clean clothes / Why was I always hungry at home / And scared of getting jumped / And our soccer goal had holes?" The answer in the hook is bitter: "Nobody is playing with the same cards / Destiny lifts its veil / Too bad / We weren't born under the same star."

T HERE'S AN ARGUMENT to be made that no French rapper has ever matched the verbal dexterity and range that you can find in the verses of classic American MCs like Nas, Biggie, Tupac, GZA or Rakim. I mean that real cutting showmanship, the dazzling shell fragment that makes American rap so pungent. In part this is due to the fact that American rappers use verbal ingenuity as a kind of evasive tool, enlisting black vernacular to stay one step ahead of accepted, assimilated "white" discourse.

But the runaway success of songs like IAM's "Petit frère" or NTM's "Laisse pas trainer ton fils" demonstrates that in France there is no schism between alternative rap and the commercial mainstream current. There is no French equivalent of artists like Immortal Technique, Mos Def or Talib Kweli; IAM and NTM never set out to "be socially conscious," as we might say in the U.S. This has given French hip-hop artists an intellectual and emotional license that can be enormously compelling. It's why the NTM rappers can growl like DMX and at the same time talk about how a father needs to love and listen to his son. On the hook of their biggest hit single Kool Shen raps, literally translated, "They shouldn't ever have to look elsewhere to find the love that should be in your eyes." You can't find a line quite like this anywhere in the Def Jam catalogue. In the big leagues of U.S. rap only Tupac could convincingly deliver this kind of sentimental sincerity, and even then it came encased in the heavy armor of thug life.

Suprême NTM was always a much harder outfit to classify, perhaps because they have been in the game the longest and are also the truest reflection of hip-hop in France. They embodied all the contradictions, circumvented all the traps. Of all the music produced in France over the last two decades, their contribution remains perhaps the most important, the most influential and the most popular among young people across all social categories. What JoeyStarr and Kool Shen gave us was the nearest possible translation of freedom—the smack of liberty that they copped by listening to the best records from the golden era of American hip-hop. They weren't flowery like Solaar, or preachy like IAM, or above the fray like Doc Gynéco. Somehow NTM nailed the anger and the cool in the same note, bypassing categories like Miles, voice in command like Rakim. They would break out dancing at shows, something virtually impossible to imagine in the world of U.S. hip-hop where the role of the MC has remained strictly verbal. They defined an entire generation and gave it a conscience. There's no way to give an account of Paris at the turn of the millennium without them.

NTM were never political in the sense of pushing a message. But they effortlessly controlled the terms of debate. The establishment attempted to paint them as dangerous and cop-hating hooligans, but one of their biggest singles, "Pose ton gun" (Put down your gun), hauntingly backed by a Bobby Womack sample, became a national anthem to nonviolence. Yet they murdered whole institutions in the space of a verse, in the turn of a rhyme. They relentlessly exposed the hypocrisy of the French establishment, the Pasqua-Debré immigration laws, censorship, political corruption and so on. When a television interviewer asked JoeyStarr about the violence of his lyrics, he corrected her. "It's not violence," he said, "*it's virulence.*" No political actor or social commentator has been as articulate about the current social impasse in France.

Desdemone Bardin, *IAM in the Studio*, 1991

With time, the rap game in France has evolved along the same lines as everywhere else. The new artists attempt to use Auto-Tune. They splurge on knock-off versions of Hype Williams videos, with interchangeable *Miami Vice* sports cars and booty girls; they abuse a plethora of mistranslated cultural references. Sefyu, the heir apparent to the hip-hop game in France today, is a morose and standoffish figure who refuses to show his face in videos and is more interested in coordinating his sneakers with his outfit than in paying for a decent beat. In a bizarre turn, Doc Gynéco veered politically to the right, infamously cheering Nicolas Sarkozy's rise to power, and reinventing himself as a cynical court jester to the elite. He told people he had grown up. But really he'd just grown into what he was all along: a jerk.

When I look at the contemporary situation, I confess it's hard not to get depressed. Nothing seems fresh anymore; nothing seems green with life or genuine yearning. Across the Atlantic come similar grumblings that hip-hop is at last postmortem. Then again, maybe I'm just older.

Hip-hop is an adolescent genre of music. Between the lines you can plainly see attempts to tackle critical issues: social inequality, sex, religion, mortality, boredom, fear. But, ungainly and awkward, it indulges in the most ridiculous immaturity. Still, the stupidity of adolescence is not without its rush, its exhilaration. Freshness has its place. The music of our youth is tinged with a special effervescence. It is imbued with meanings we can only barely articulate, colored with feelings couched in half-remembered conversations, in old friends and half-forgotten crushes, stored amid all the whirring dynamos of the unconscious. Maybe this is why on a personal level French hip-hop is so easy for me to forgive, even though it still has a kind of embarrassing stigma. French hip-hop? *Really?* Well, yes. I actually can't listen to JoeyStarr shouting out, *"Saint-Denis Saint-Denis Funk Funky-Fresh!"* without cracking a huge smile. *Saint-Denis, c'est de la bombe bébé!*

But emotional immaturity doesn't imply historical insignificance. If we could borrow Zola's eyeglasses and look down on the city of Paris to take stock of the last two decades, what would instantly stand out is a series of kaleidoscopic collisions seething with energy and frustration: the banlieues, the stalemate of the ghetto, the restless periphery of the marginalized sons and daughters of the postwar immigration and their uncertain fate. Hip-hop has registered and encoded this historical narrative and expressed it in a native tongue.

> *Tout n'est pas si facile,*
> *Les destins se séparent, l'amitié c'est fragile*
> *Pour nous la vie ne fut jamais un long fleuve tranquille*

Desdemone Bardin, *DJ Dee Nasty Radio Nova*, 1991

Nothing is so easy,
Destinies separate us, friendship is fragile
For us life was never a long tranquil river

When I hear Kool Shen rap on lost friendships it pulls me back to a certain time and a certain place. It wasn't easy for anyone. But we were all there and hip-hop was our music; and because we were adolescents it was also our conscience. Now when the beat flows and I nod my head, the grain of Kool Shen's voice still has the power to evoke certain truths. It's hard coming up in the world. You have the best of times and the best of friends. Then things fall apart. Or maybe things just change. You grow older and you don't always figure shit out. Ralph Ellison defined the blues as "an impulse to keep the painful details and episodes of a brutal experience alive in one's aching consciousness, to finger its jagged grain." Hip-hop is steeped in this sensibility. The verbal dexterity, the allusive sampling, the poses and the braggadocio, they all amount to one underlying message: *I rock the mic—life's a bitch, and then you die*. It's about snatching good times from the teeth of times that couldn't be worse. Life is not a tranquil river. It's like that, and that's the way it is.

T**HE WAY IT** is. The Caroline I knew from the days of MC Solaar, who danced with me all night at my first boum and looked prettier in a dress than Sophie Marceau, dated a drug dealer. She lived in London for a while. She dropped in and out of design schools. She moved to Milan with a new boyfriend who she found on Myspace. Years went by, college. We sent each other messages, emails sometimes. The last time I saw her she was hung over and embarrassed. She looked very beautiful. We didn't talk about music. We didn't really talk about anything. She doesn't know that when I hear MC Solaar's song "Caroline" I still think of her. It wouldn't mean anything anyway. The last time I saw her was in the summer of 2008. NTM officially split up in 2001, but they decided to reassemble one last time to play a live farewell show. 1988-2008: the end of an era. The show was the hype of the town. I asked Caroline if she wanted to go. She gave me the same vacant stare she gave years ago and ducked the invitation. She asked me if I intended to see them. I said I was thinking about it, but I knew the truth was I would never go.

All images taken from screenshots of *Watch Dogs*

WATCH DOGS

by Steven Poole

THERE IS A revealing moment in *No Place to Hide*, Glenn Greenwald's account of the NSA revelations, when hacker-whistleblower Edward Snowden explains how he has learned some of his moral lessons from videogames. In videogames, Snowden says, "The protagonist is often an ordinary person, who finds himself faced with grave injustices from powerful forces and has the choice to flee in fear or to fight for his beliefs." As though to return the compliment, the recent videogame *Watch Dogs*, published by Ubisoft and developed under creative director Jonathan Morin, is set in a near future of omnipresent electronic surveillance and features as its protagonist a brilliant hacker fighting powerful forces.

The hacker is named Aiden Pearce, and he talks, as is the fashion in action movies, in a gravelly whisper that would be perfectly inaudible at normal speaking distance. (The voice actor, Noam Jenkins, seems to be channeling Christian Bale as Batman.) Pearce lives in "hideouts" across Chicago: these dens, whether motel rooms or shipping containers, always contain multiple glowing LCD monitors. He will project a clue-marked map of the city onto a wall, and then punch the wall to exhibit frustration. Later in the game he is joined by a woman hacker with facial piercings, a mohican ponytail and a pixelated skull on her black t-shirt. She is not explicitly called the "Girl with the Dragon Tattoo," but she might as well be. Pearce represents a more grungified version of the hacker-hero than the preppy Snowden (he sleeps in his baseball cap, trench coat and boots, and never brushes his teeth in the morning), but he is definitely fighting rather than fleeing, a moral stand that Snowden admires in other videogames. After a hacking heist went wrong, someone killed Pearce's niece. Now he's out for justice.

That Pearce is a hacker is fundamental to the game's unique selling point, because *Watch Dogs* is the first videogame to provide a widely explorable simulation of an urban environment that is itself, within the fiction, extensively computer-controlled, and so can be taken over by a tech wiz with a customized smartphone. Underneath the extraordinarily detailed and all-but-photorealistic simulation of Chicago that provides the game's primary environment is a second-order virtual city that is visualized in gorgeous monochrome geometric

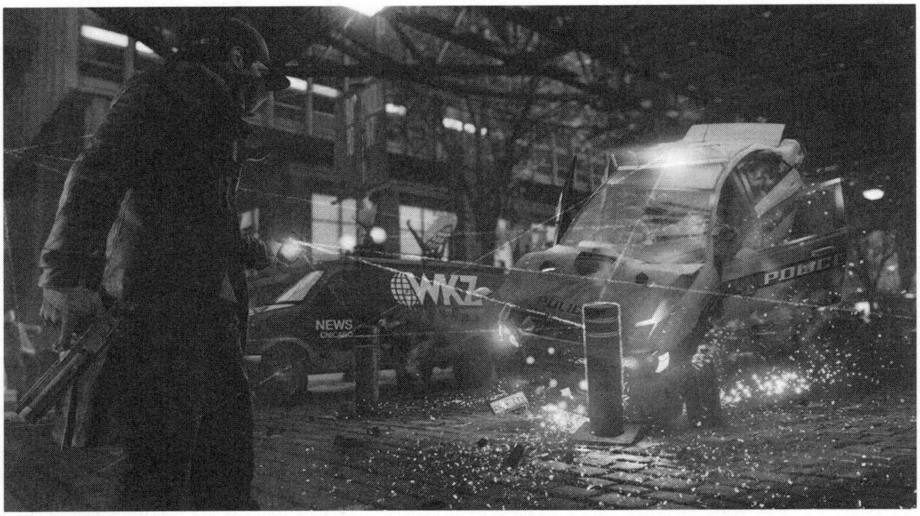
WKZ
NEWS
POLICE

wireframe, reminiscent of William Gibson's earliest descriptions of cyberspace. This is known as ctOS: Chicago's "central operating system."

The metacybernetics of these twin nested simulations are rich: in this virtual Chicago, not only are the CCTV cameras, traffic lights and soda machines computerized, but so are the bridges, shipping cranes and "L" trains. All are potential tools for creating municipal mayhem for the inventive hacker, who can even take down the grid and cause a complete blackout over several blocks. Much of the game is spent chasing or being chased in cars, furnishing much potential for emergent B-movie moments. To shake off police vehicles, Pearce can hack a bridge so that it begins to rise the moment he drives onto it, allowing his car to leap the gap and leave the cops behind. (Whatever his other transgressions, Pearce may rest assured that no one will ever pull him over for dangerous driving, no matter if he careens up over curbs, smashes through telegraph poles or speeds into oncoming traffic.)

In a way *Watch Dogs* thus stands as a critique of modern urbanism's ideal of the "smart city," in which infrastructure is controlled by and reports to networked information technology. The "smarter" the city gets in this sense, the more vulnerable it becomes to the geek with a grudge. What Pearce says about a prison he infiltrates at one point in order to intimidate a witness—that he couldn't possibly do what he wants if it weren't a computerized correctional facility—applies all the more to the game's entire world.

At its best, in its kinetic demonstrations of power over the articulated urban skeleton of concrete and steel, *Watch Dogs* creates the compelling illusion that one can bend an entire city to one's will—as long as, that is, one's will is aligned with the protagonist's prescripted capabilities, rather than nurturing any more nuanced ambitions. One may hack electronic road signs, but only so as to show fellow motorists one of a handful of canned paranoia nuggets ("It's a trap!"; "Gotta believe it to see it"). There is no option to leave a few lines of Fernando Pessoa's poetry as pensive roadside graffiti. Which is all the more to be regretted since—as is common in the "open world" genre of large-arena videogames—arguably the most potent moments in *Watch Dogs* are those when one is not really doing anything.

As with the *Grand Theft Auto* series, which also attempts to build virtual copies of real cities in spectacular, all-too-solid detail, one of the most pleasant things one can do in *Watch Dogs* is simply to be a flâneur. On foot, on a motorbike, in a car, or on one of many handily abandoned motorboats, one may cruise around, observing the changing light in the sky and watching the simulated street life go by. On several occasions this writer pulled over to admire the view of downtown Chicago as seen from over the water during a hazy sunrise. To drive around the city at dusk with russet autumn leaves waving in the trees and downbeat electronica pumping from the car stereo is a deep pleasure in itself, as though one is participating in an interactive outtake from a Michael Mann film.

The problem with *Watch Dogs*, as with *Grand Theft Auto* and all other examples of the urban-sandbox genre, is that the videogame's pre-programmed landscape of possibility and risk relentlessly pushes the player instead into a murder-spree *dérive*. One is not permitted to go into stores (except, here and there, a gun shop); it is impossible to sit down on a park bench. Pearce cannot go to a museum or the cinema—he never even eats. Accidentally mowing down a few pedestrians in one's car, on the other hand, comes with no real consequences, and if one is chased by the police it is the path of least resistance within the logic of the game to start shooting rather than continuing to evade them. ("Police homicide," reads the bland pop-up message in *Watch Dogs*; "-1 point reputation.") Unlike *Grand Theft Auto*, moreover, *Watch Dogs* actively encourages the player to harm ordinary citizens in invisible ways, by compromising their cell-phone banking apps and stealing their money. What its behavioral repertoire mostly boils down to, then, is psychotic flânerie plus neatly virtualized mugging.

This is possible because the citizens of this lovingly modeled Chicago themselves turn out to be just as hackable as the city's infrastructure. "I'll have to thank ctOS one day," Pearce whisper-growls. "A simple breach of their facial-recognition software and I've got access to everyone's personal details." Not only is the player encouraged to steal citizens' money, but bite-sized information about their financial difficulties, hobbies and emotional issues is portrayed in floating information cards above their heads: "suffers from claustrophobia," "collects cans and bottles," and so forth. Pearce thus enjoys an even more intimate version of the panoptical powers that Edward Snowden has described having had as an NSA contractor. "You could read anyone's email in the world," Snowden explained. "Anybody you've got an email address for, any website you can watch traffic to and from it, any computer that an individual sits at you can watch it, any laptop that you're tracking you can follow it as it moves from place to place throughout the world." (We now know that staffers at the NSA and other agencies passed around people's sexts for office entertainment. Thankfully, *Watch Dogs* does not go as far as to feature naked camera-phone snaps of its invented people.)

But whereas Snowden was outraged that anyone could have such power, Aiden Pearce revels in it—at least when it's his. At one point, he discovers that the city is recording people inside their own homes, and expresses disapproval: "ctOS filming these people and they have no idea," he complains, sotto voce. Then he is back out on the street, hacking everyone's cell-phone conversations and text messages, and stealing from their bank accounts. All the more peculiar, then, that the game also offers optional "vigilante" crime-fighting missions:

thanks to one's relentless intrusions into the private lives of the citizenry, one is sometimes alerted to the imminent commission of an assault or theft, and given the option to foil it by beating up the malefactor with a telescopic baton. To judge the point at which a potential criminal becomes an actual criminal who has not quite yet committed his crime, however, is a subtle matter indeed, and the player is often punished for erring on the side of pre-emption—even though the hacked information that has led the player to the criminal is presumptively, within the fiction, 100 percent accurate. This is *Minority Report* without the moral complexity.

Pearce's powers, which make him a smartphone-toting god able to see into the souls of everyone and know their darkest secrets, are also employed by the game's scenarists to justify the frequent descents into mass killing, when the hero must storm one of many facilities staffed by ctOS guards. Here the game becomes merely a second-rate imitator of military-simulations-cum-Michael-Bay-movies such as the *Call of Duty* series. Since Pearce is not a soldier, and his adversaries are not bomb-throwing Islamists or invading Russians, his serial murdering of ctOS security workers is narratively excused by the fact that, according to their hacked pop-up biographies, they are all criminals-at-large, guilty of everything from fraud to sexual assault. But would ctOS itself not have been able to dig up these secrets? And if so, would it not probably have preferred to screen out such evidently undesirable employees? If the player stops to wonder for too long about such awkward questions, she will probably just get shot in the face and be obliged to reload the mission.

The game's most ingenious and novel moments are far removed from the general ambience of psychotic flânerie and criminal crimefighting. They are the elaborate spatial puzzles that the player must solve for Pearce to hack in to the next ctOS tower—a kind of antenna that functions as a neural node of the city's electronic brain. One becomes disembodied, leaping from one CCTV camera to another in order to discover the sequence of junction boxes and switches that, once hacked, will lead to the core. (That one requires line of sight to the next object in order to hack it is a patently unrealistic restriction, but it is necessary to create the arena for such mental acrobatics.) In these quiet and cerebral sequences, one adopts a multiple and fluid view—analogous to the "view from nowhere" described by the philosopher Thomas Nagel—insofar as it stands outside any subjective perspective but is able to encompass them all. One is first-person singular and first-person plural; one is pure mind, traveling at will. Here is an inventive and satisfying translation into three-dimensional riddles of the old saw that information is power. It is only when one finally attains the tower's core that proceedings revert to a surprisingly ancient puzzle-videogame paradigm in which one has to rotate junctions to cause current to flow the right way through a circuit. At bottom, the hacker-hero's feats of magic depend on a simple question of information plumbing. Yet perhaps that is appropriate, since as we know from life as well as electronic fiction, information plumbing will always spring leaks.

Watch Dogs presents a Hollywoodized version of hacking, suffers from a derivative, cliché-ridden and often nonsensical script, and asks the player to admire and abet a flatly psychopathic avenger for whom no "collateral" body-count is too high. It is, in other words, a modern high-budget videogame. Yet its picture of omnipresent personal surveillance is the most consistent yet attempted in this medium, and is at times authentically disturbing. One ingenious "social" (or rather anti-social) feature, moreover, cleverly turns players against one another, allowing them to hack into each other's worlds. The hero must then identify the human malefactor among the simulated urbanites within a strict time limit. Who on this sidewalk is not behaving like a computer-controlled character—or, perhaps, too much like one? The first time this happens, at least, it generates a visceral sense of paranoia and fear of intrusion from any quarter. (After one or two such experiences, one is glad to switch off the interruptions.) Given the potency of such moments and the beauty of its pure information-space enigmas, it is clear that the game could have been a truly courageous departure for the form if only the player had been given no access at all to guns, homemade bombs and the rest of the stereotypical videogame arsenal. What if, in other words, Aiden Pearce's only weapons—like those of Edward Snowden—were his computers and his intelligence?

As it is, the most contrarian thing one can do in *Watch Dogs* is to refuse to pursue any of the scripted missions at all. There is plenty of space for virtual tourism and even civic education—one may, for instance, "check in" at various Chicago landmarks to learn more about their history. A true rebel player of the game, perhaps, will simply drive around the bejeweled nighttime city in a sensible hybrid vehicle, carefully observing the speed limit and admiring the looming gray mass and soft yellow illumination of office buildings, while perhaps occasionally taking a voyeuristic peek into the life of a passing pedestrian. This is eerier and more moodily compelling than anything the game wants the player to do. For an hour or two, it is even enough.

THE GREAT GATSBY
F. Scott Fitzgerald
1925

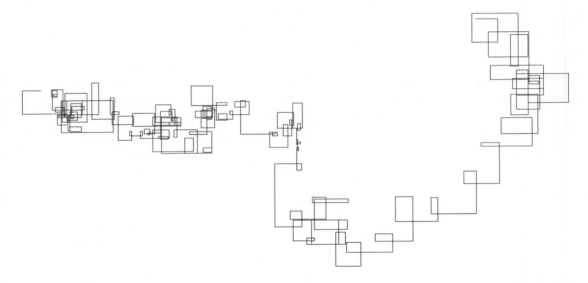

Stefanie Posavec, all images are from the *First Chapters* series, 2011

DISTANT READING

by Scott Esposito

EVERY DECADE SINCE the 1950s, a literary doctrine or two has dominated the academy. In the Sixties it was structuralism and reader response theory; in the Seventies, deconstruction. The Eighties saw the emergence of New Historicism and cultural studies; and the Nineties gave us a canon-smashing smörgåsbord of postcolonialism, feminist theory and gender studies. The Aughts proudly declared the end of theory, but the declaration proved to be premature. In this second decade of the new millennium we are seeing the emergence of a new tool for cracking open the text and telling the story of the novel. It is custom-built for a world where information comes not from an encyclopedia but from a Google search, and it partakes in an aspiration legible to the techno-utopians whispering Big Data. This fat little tuber grown off the back of the digital humanities is none other than Franco Moretti's *distant reading*.

Moretti has ridden his doctrine to rock star status—such astonishing cultural capital that Stanford gave him a whole "literary lab" while most humanities professors scrape by on scraps. Though he no more invented distant reading than did Bill Gates invent the graphic user interface, Moretti has, like the software pioneer, grabbed a monopoly share of the credit. Distant reading is perhaps best thought of as the culminating stroke in that century-long process reversing the hegemony of the New Critics. Whereas their close reading consolidated the practice of scrutinizing a single passage, which every student now learns to do as a teenager, distant reading instead sifts through *everything* from afar, looking for patterns and clues in the aggregate.

Moretti is primarily an academic, which means his primary purpose is to produce knowledge for other academics. That said, his prose and the stories he tells about his data may speak to anyone who cares about literature. For instance, "Style, Inc.," one of Moretti's best-known and most interesting studies to date, charts how the average length of novel titles declined from roughly fifteen words in the 1750s to just six words in the 1790s—and then, by the nineteenth century, to just a word or three (think *Jane Eyre*, *Middlemarch*, all those Dickens and Balzac novels). Looking closer, Moretti finds a full-scale narrative carrying us through the nineteenth century—style and the market engorging upon one another and spinning off new sorts of titles that make for new sorts of novels: first the abstract title (e.g. *Sense and Sensibility*), which conditioned readers to believe that novels should move teleologically toward a final point; and then the metaphorical title (*Heart of Darkness*), which revealed a text's central "ideology" like a seductive flash of thigh right on the book's cover. Just by looking at titles, Moretti is able to sketch an entire shadow history of the novel's rise, culminating with a fascinating theory on what might distinguish the nineteenth-century novel from the twentieth:

> By the end of the [nineteenth] century [titular metaphors] are everywhere (*The Belly of Paris*; *The Doll*; *Ghosts*; *The Octopus*; *Heart of Darkness*; *The Beast in the Jungle*), so they must have taken root sometime in the third quarter of the nineteenth century, and the glimpses one gets suggest a lot of hesitation on the part of writers: Gaskell shifting at the last minute from *Margaret Hale* to *North and South* (proper name to metaphor); Dickens doing the opposite, from *Nobody's Fault* to *Little Dorrit*. Announcing a story with a metaphor must have seemed strange—and it is strange: if abstractions are removed from the plot, then metaphors are twice removed: interpretations that *require an interpretation*, as it were. But it is precisely this "difficulty" of metaphors that holds the secret of the title-as-ad. Eighteenth-century summaries told readers a lot of things about the novel, yes; but they never really engaged their intelligence. And instead, by puzzling and challenging readers, metaphors induced them to take an active interest in the novel from the very first word. If you are trying to sell a product, that's exactly what you want.

This is great stuff, even if it's not exactly *sui generis*. Seen from a wide historical perspective, Moretti's distant reading looks a lot like structuralism minus all those lusty paeans to the pleasure of the text. Recall that Claude Lévi-Strauss discovered patterns by sifting through the world's myths, and Roland Barthes taught us that these very same patterns were played out in local wrestling matches and soap advertisements. Moretti clearly builds on such traditions, updating his methods for a time when data capture is becoming indispensible to our way of life, like an omnipresent machine that we're not sure we wanted to turn on but certainly can't turn off: everything from the mindboggling databases that allow Amazon to ship millions of different goods, to the energy grids that keep the lights on, to the schedules that organize the world's flights (and the scanners that warn who should be kept off of them)—even the algorithms that let you sort through carriers and routes to purchase the lowest-priced ticket.

Which is to say, Moretti's technique is important in part because we're ready to receive it. It was not always so. When the New Critics did their pioneering work, close reading made sense. It was an intuitive technique to generations raised on Bible study, and there was an authoritative set of texts that anyone

FIRST CHAPTERS

Sentence drawings of first chapters from 20th-century British and American literature

WORD COUNT *

⫿ 1 word
⫿⫿ 5 words
⫿⫿⫿ 10 words
⫿⫿⫿⫿⫿⫿⫿⫿⫿⫿⫿⫿⫿⫿⫿⫿ 100 words

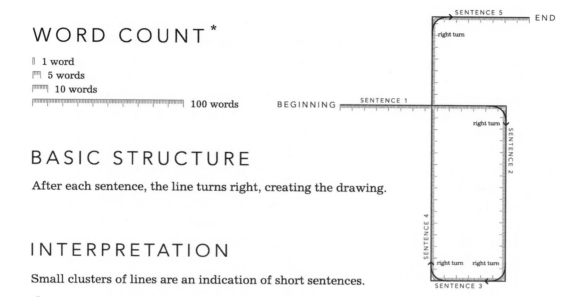

BEGINNING

SENTENCE 1

SENTENCE 2

SENTENCE 3

SENTENCE 4

SENTENCE 5

END

right turn

right turn

right turn   right turn

BASIC STRUCTURE

After each sentence, the line turns right, creating the drawing.

INTERPRETATION

Small clusters of lines are an indication of short sentences.

A loose drawing with longer lines indicates a chapter with many long sentences.

A drawing that moves consistently around the same area means that all the sentences have a similar word count.

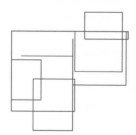

---

* The lines on this key are not to scale

aspiring to be "well read" might hope to consume in a lifetime. Later generations added nuances appropriate to their own eras: as the structuralists gained
currency, they declared that any canon was just a reflection of power imbalances
based in our politics and economy; later, as minorities, women and the queer
community took their share of academic authority, they tore the white-male
canon to shreds. Herein we see the roots of distant reading: the content of the
books is still important, but the conversation starts to move beyond the text. By
the time we get to New Historicism, postcolonialism et al., there is an entirely
new orthodoxy: everywhere you look is a text ripe for analysis, and it's no longer
radical to suggest that everyday anecdotes are just as worthy of scholarly attention as Shakespeare. Anyone who grants undue importance to the latter—like
Harold Bloom and his 26-author Western canon—is a living anachronism.

Insofar as there is something genuinely new in Moretti, it has to do with
what Big Data is now doing to our concepts of quality and authority. We've
all read enough customer reviews to know that the institutionalized critic is a
diminished concept. And we also know that the explosion of computing power
available to the average person has curtailed the authority of gatekeepers. Yes,
the *New York Times* is still the *New York Times*, but its authority has been eroded
by a horde of Lilliputians. Technology allowed this, just as it has permitted statistics to become a measure of quality. Witness the low sales figures that now
follow mid-list authors around like a contagious disease; that self-perpetuating
prophecy known as the Amazon sales rank; the cult of Nate Silver; the citation
of download figures as a measure of an app's success; the count of retweets
and Facebook shares that now appears on every conceivable web page; the ther-
monuclear explosion of lists of all varieties on the web. Metrics have become
radicalized elsewhere, too, from No Child Left Behind's obsessive insistence on
test scores to Walmart's quantification of its employees' daily performance.

"It felt like the entire history of literature could be rewritten in a new vein,"
Moretti has written of his essay "The Slaughterhouse of Literature," where he
first used data to put his "falsifiable" theories to the test. Data, Moretti believed,
could end longstanding arguments or upset orthodoxies. It might reveal a new
history of the novel, a whole new geography of literature. And Moretti is, unlike
most literary critics, a natural with numbers. The childlike glee he takes in his
charts and diagrams is clear to anyone who takes a moment to read his work.
But the most important thing that numbers do for Moretti is answer new kinds
of questions. He makes the point clear in *Graphs, Maps, Trees*: the corpus he
wants to tackle is so gigantic that, even if we read "a novel a day every day of
the year," this work "would take a century or so." A man with such aspirations
needs machines.

But what sorts of revolutionary narratives does he wish to unveil? For one thing, Moretti is a formalist. He cares about books not for their plots or characters but because they can tell us secrets about the world that produced them. Likewise, he cares about grammar because he finds understanding the syntax of a given age akin to understanding the age itself. In *Distant Reading* he calls what he does "formalism without close reading," borrowing the phrase from literary theorist Jonathan Arac; this involves "identifying a discrete formal trait and then following its metamorphoses through a whole series of texts." Moretti is also a historian, to a much greater degree than most other people considered literary theorists: in *The Bourgeois* he flatly tells us that he's interested in writers like Defoe and Ibsen because they allow "the past to recover its voice." And how does the past speak to us? "*Only* through the medium of forms." Distant reading turns distance into "not an obstacle but a specific form of knowledge: fewer elements, hence a sharper sense of their overall interconnection. Shapes, relations, structures. Forms. Models."

These are the things Moretti cares about. In *Atlas of the European Novel* he tells us, "What quantitative methods have to offer the historians of literature [is] a reversal of the hierarchy between the exception and the series, where the latter becomes—as it is—the true protagonist of cultural life. A history of literature as a history *of norms.*" That is, a history of literature where it is not the individual that dominates but the structure, not *Jane Eyre* but the bildungsroman. It is in this connection that he often draws on biological evolution for concepts and terminology, frequently citing Charles Darwin and Stephen Jay Gould. Likewise, he professes admiration for the Russian formalist par excellence Viktor Shklovsky, who ascribed an uncertain, at times haphazard, trajectory to the development of the novel, and whom Moretti reminds us said that literature develops via a "canonization of the cadet branch."

As that last quote implies, Moretti likes to play up his fixation on what he repeatedly terms the "periphery," and what we'd call, in the faddish language of today, "the long tail." This may be a physical periphery—like all those far off European countries ignored when we study Dickens and Austen—but it can just as well be a literary one, like those reams of middling detective fiction that Arthur Conan Doyle effectively put to dust. Of course, there is a good reason the periphery tends to be ignored by most critics: its quality as literature is low, something even Moretti readily admits. Which leads us to a strange fact about Moretti—as invested as he is in counter-narratives, his new findings tend to enshrine the same old books. In one of his many moments of enthusiasm for the overlooked, Moretti quotes Hegel's downright Rumsfeldian pronouncement that "the *well*-known in general, being well-known, is actually *not* known." Thus

A ROOM OF ONE'S OWN
Virginia Woolf
1929

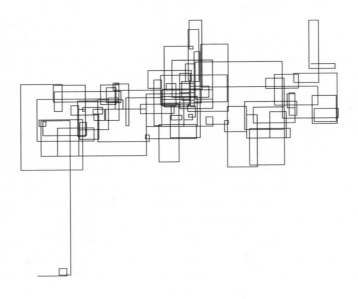

Moretti combs through every last ignored detective novel he can find in order, ultimately, to better understand the success of Sherlock Holmes. Or take his most recent book, *The Bourgeois*, which he says is "a dialogue between Defoe and Weber." He isn't out to discover writers to replace Defoe and Weber; he just wants to understand them better, and with them, that most commonplace of all literary classes, the middle class. The pages of his studies are dominated by names familiar to all: *Hamlet*, Dickens, Austen, *Buddenbrooks*, *Don Quixote*, Balzac and so on.

There is therefore a curious reaffirmation of the status quo in Moretti's work. True, he often starts his analysis in the periphery, but time and time again he ends up right back where traditional literary critics start. There are no little-known additions to the canon in Moretti's work, no elimination of pretenders, no rediscovered genres or hidden gems. None of this. Unlike many of his iconoclastic forebears in literary theory, Moretti attempts to give us new narratives about why the center is central.

In a sense, then, distant reading is another of those data-driven technologies that merely *promises* to threaten existing sources of power. I do not deny that Big Data still offers the best shot at disruption that we have at the moment. The collective known as Anonymous, Nate Silver's FiveThirtyEight, and even Barack Obama's first presidential campaign have all used data to bring new perspectives into the public consciousness. But for the most part Big Data has been co-opted by the empowered, just like various promising technologies before it: radio, film, telephone, television and audio/video recorders. Moretti claims that, by bringing the benefits of data to literature, he is speaking up for the forgotten—the uncounted libraries of ignored books that no one has ever bothered to submit to literary analysis. His argument hinges on the idea that literature should benefit from technology and science because that's what's going on in so many other spheres of society. But is it really so clear that technology is *benefitting* these other spheres?

Moreover, Moretti sometimes fails to recognize that literature is a very strange place. Our theorist may give the impression that it is a backwards field that needs a technological tune-up, but the inconvenient truth is that literature is out of step because it really *is* different. Perhaps this is why Moretti's inquiries tend to start with data, but his conclusions are hardly more scientific than those of any other theorist. Most of the time he seems aware of this, carefully arguing from well-founded premises and tip-toeing around the fact that he's not really a scientist. He rarely attempts to disprove the ideas of his fellow theorists, and it's a good thing, because literary studies doesn't function like a science, where one experiment can shatter orthodoxies and enshrine a new order. Although there are better and worse responses, there is no definitive response to any given text:

A FAREWELL TO ARMS
Ernest Hemingway
1937

INTRUDER IN THE DUST
William Faulkner
1948

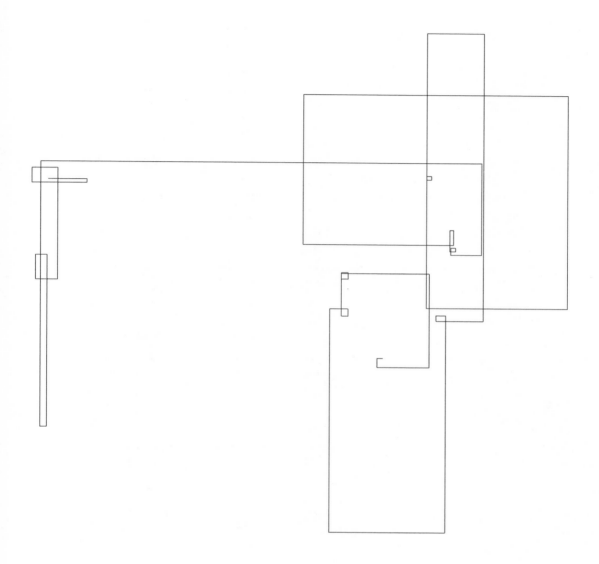

a brilliant analysis of Balzac, for instance, can inspire my own interpretation without rendering it obsolete.

IN SCIENCE, ACCESS to better data counts: the Large Hadron Collider tells us more about our world than weaker supercolliders; bigger telescopes and more sensitive instruments can solve questions previously considered unanswerable; even in a social science like economics, having more and better data can often yield more convincing results. Not so with literary criticism. One of Moretti's favorite, most relied-upon studies, Erich Auerbach's *Mimesis*, was written while the author was marooned in Istanbul during World War II, far away from almost all his favorite works of Western literature. Indeed we might say that this classic was made possible by the radical *contraction* of the data available to its author. Likewise, Northrop Frye's *Anatomy of Criticism* is a brilliant, compelling work, no matter that it's based almost completely on the writing of dead white men and that its scientific theory of literature has been declared obsolete.

It may be that all great work is based on hubris, and Moretti's is simply more obvious than most. I admit that I get weak in the knees when Moretti talks about "the role of the gerund in *Robinson Crusoe*," but I in no way expect that the story he tells will refute all the other stories told about *Crusoe*. Moreover, its worth has less to do with the amount of data Moretti feeds into a computer than it does with his capacity to articulate what he finds. No man who writes prose like this could truly disbelieve in close reading, or claim that every question has its answer:

> There is something ghostly, in this history where questions disappear, and answers survive. But if we accept the idea of literary forms as the fossil remains of what had once been a living and problematic present; and if we work our way backwards, "reverse-engineering" it to understand the problem it was designed to solve; if we do this, then formal analysis may unlock—in principle, if not always in practice—a dimension of the past that would otherwise be hidden. Here lies its possible contribution to historical knowledge: by understanding the opacity of Ibsen's hints to the past, or the oblique semantics of Victorian adjectives, or even (at first sight, not a cheerful task) the role of the gerund in *Robinson Crusoe*, we enter a realm of shadows, where the past recovers its voice, and still speaks to us.

It is beyond doubt that reading will change with technology, and Moretti has ample incentive to cheerlead such developments: his generous funding and star position, not to mention his professional reputation, is premised on them. But it may be no accident that he comments very little on the enormous questions that his methods stir up. For all his talk about dragging literary criticism into the digital era, in *The Bourgeois* he admits that he cannot relate the insights he makes about the rise of the novel to contemporary problems. This is a lament that hangs over all his work. Yes, his data is big, but it is also old: the verb patterns of *Robinson Crusoe*, the concentration of publishing in nineteenth-century Europe, the character geography of *Hamlet*. Taken individually, Moretti's books and papers tell us much about history, but his only grand *idea* appears to be that data is the future of literary studies.

But perhaps Moretti's work *will* help young critics see how data can be used to address new questions about today's authors. One example of a satisfying fusion of Moretti's methods and contemporary concerns—Ed Finn's essay "Becoming Yourself: The Afterlife of Reception"—uses Amazon's recommendation algorithm to construct a data set around the books of David Foster Wallace; it also uses data sets made from professional reviews of Wallace in national newspapers and customer reviews from Amazon. Based on these, Finn uncovers ways in which readers viewed the alleged postmodernist differently from his peers. For instance, he finds that, whereas the critics most often liken him to a familiar clique (e.g. Pynchon, Barth and DeLillo), the everyday readers make different comparisons: *Ulysses*, *Moby-Dick* and (most surprisingly) *Les Misérables*. Whereas critics see Wallace in terms of his postmodernist peers, readers see him in terms of the Great Books. In turning Moretti's methods to such an analysis, Finn raises important questions: Why do we consider Wallace so original? Whose appreciation of him is most valid? And who now holds the most authority—computers, critics or consumers?

Not that long ago, the answer to that final question would have been obvious. The literary doctrines that have emerged in the past few decades have made it much more of a debate, as have changes in the texture of culture and communications. Teasing out the consequences of these changes will be an important part of discovering the novel's place in the twenty-first century. Moretti has played a substantial role in advancing this conversation (Finn notes him as an inspiration for "Becoming Yourself"), but his work looks backwards, not forwards. Perhaps a new generation of writers will ask the questions his methods only hint at.

ART SPIEGELMAN & PHILLIP JOHNSTON
WORDLESS!
RAW
NOW IT'S SAFE FOR ADULTS
TO READ COMMIX!
ART SPIEGELMAN
presents picture stories by
FRANS MASEREEL,
H.M. BATEMAN,
LYND WARD, OTTO NUCKEL,
MILT GROSS, SI LEWEN
plus his own new work
"SHAPING THOUGHT!"
with music by
PHILLIP JOHNSTON

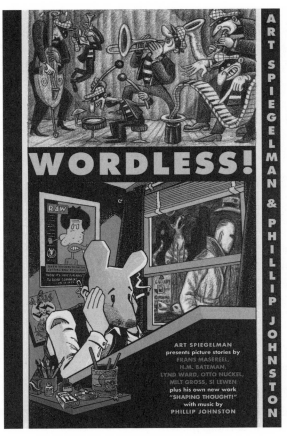

"Wordless!" poster, 2013

WORDLESS!

by Tim Peters

ART SPIEGELMAN'S MAUS is a nearly 300-page-long, autobiographical comic about both surviving the Holocaust and surviving being the child of survivors of the Holocaust—where the Jews are depicted as mice, the Nazis as cats, the Poles as pigs and the Americans as dogs. When it was published in 1991, *Maus* became a surprise bestseller and was awarded a *sui generis* Pulitzer Prize. It also brought into popular parlance the term "graphic novel," which had been deployed more than a decade earlier by the cartoonist Will Eisner to designate serious, literate, long-form comics without bringing along the baggage attached to the word "comics."

Comics have never held much prestige. Full-color newspaper comics in the 1890s were the equivalent of today's Angry Birds or FarmVille—a newfangled, hyperactive form of entertainment meant to appeal to the lowest common denominator: to kids, to immigrants, to the uneducated working class. In fact, the phrase "yellow journalism" can be traced back to a character called the Yellow Kid who appeared in the newspaper comic strips that both William Randolph Hearst and Joseph Pulitzer were publishing as part of their Gilded Age circulation wars. After World War II, the massive popularity of comic books (which had evolved out of the newspaper comic strip) led a psychiatrist named Fredric Wertham to warn that they were depraving the youth of America. His book *Seduction of the Innocent* (1954) inspired public burnings of comic books and the creation of the Comics Code, which stiffened and sterilized the medium just as the Hays Code had sterilized Hollywood.

The underground, self-published comics of the Sixties and Seventies—those of R. Crumb or Gilbert Shelton or Bill Griffith, or of Spiegelman himself—attempted to make comics seem daring and edgy and intended for an older reader. (The admonition on *Zap Comix* No. 1 is "Fair warning: for adult intellectuals only!") But these comics had a reputation of being tawdry and crude, populated with characters who were exaggerated and grotesque and therefore still "cartoonish." A breakthrough came in 1972, when a cartoonist named Justin Green, in a fugue of guilt-stricken catharsis, created a 44-page-long autobiographical comic book called *Binky Brown Meets the Holy Virgin Mary*. The story is about Green's childhood as a tortured Catholic, and how his religion-induced scrupulosity turned into full-on OCD. (At one point, he imagines his fingers and toes have sprouted penises, all of which emit a beam of unholy sexual energy that he can't let intersect with or shine upon any sort of Catholic iconography). With *Binky Brown*, comics entered the mirror stage: they could all of a sudden be used for self-reflection and self-analysis, for an author to have an illustrated conversation with himself through the panels on the page. The ground was cleared for a new kind of comic: complex, self-conscious and demanding. "Without *Binky Brown*, there would be no *Maus*," Spiegelman once wrote.

MAUS WAS SO successful that it crippled Spiegelman artistically. As he said in 2002, "After *Maus*, I just felt that there were eyeballs mounted on my shoulder at all times, and that made it paralyzing." In lieu of making comics, Spiegelman has spent much of the past twenty-plus years lecturing about their history. Some of these lectures are overviews —as he calls it, his "Comix 101" survey—and some of them are specific, like the ones on Chester Gould (the creator of *Dick Tracy*) or Harvey Kurtzman (one of the cofounders of *Mad*). They're part of what Spiegelman refers to as the "Faustian deal" he's been brokering with the guardians and gatekeepers of upper-echelon American culture. As he said in *MetaMaus*, his 2011 memoir about the making of *Maus*: "If comics are to survive for another century, once they're no longer a part of the most-mass part of mass culture, they've got to redefine themselves as Art or die." This redefinition has entailed comics being shown on the walls of contemporary art museums like the MoMA, the MCA Chicago and the Hammer Museum; comic artists receiving awards like the MacArthur and the Guggenheim and being interviewed for a new "Art of Comics" section in the *Paris Review*; and the whole thing being the subject of scholarly monographs and multi-day academic conferences.

The most august of these academic conferences to date was held in 2012 at the University of Chicago's Logan Center for the Arts, the centerpiece of which is a soaring tower whose exterior can readily be described as "ivory." The conference, "Comics: Philosophy and Practice," brought together the heroes of the 1960s underground (R. Crumb, Spiegelman, Justin Green and others) with present-day graphic novel auteurs (Dan Clowes, Chris Ware, Seth and others). Shunned from the discussion was anyone having anything to do with superhero comic books or mainstream newspaper comic strips, no matter how respected or popular their work. Alan Moore (*Watchmen*), Frank Miller (*The Dark Knight Returns*), Patrick McDonnell (*Mutts*) and Bill Watterson (*Calvin and Hobbes*) were not included.

Art Spiegelman speaking at the Wexner Center for the Arts at OSU
Photo by A. J. Zanyk

It was at this same Logan Center for the Arts that Spiegelman, in January of this year, put on "Wordless!," an "intellectual vaudeville" and "lowbrow Chautauqua" that consists of a multimedia art-history lecture accompanied by a jazz sextet. The history lecture focuses on a short-lived, early twentieth-century artistic/literary phenomenon known as the wordless or woodcut novel, which Spiegelman argues is the original graphic novel and the progenitor of *Maus*. As he says early on in "Wordless!," "I've been called the father of the graphic novel, but I'm here today demanding a blood test." Aside from the woodcut novel, Spiegelman talks about a number of silent comics (comics that have no dialogue) and about his own career in cartooning. Every so often he steps offstage and allows the sextet to take over while a montage of scenes from the wordless novels or comics he was just discussing plays overhead. If you've ever seen a silent film with live orchestral accompaniment, "Wordless!" sort of feels like that—which is appropriate, given that many of the artists who made these wordless novels were influenced by silent cinema and that their books were essentially movie screens that you could hold in your hands.

The first woodcut novel was created by a Flemish artist named Frans Masereel just after World War I. In 1918 he published a book called *25 Images de la Passion d'un Homme* (*The Passion of a Man*), which tells a story through black-and-white woodcuts. There's one image per page (but only on the right side of each two-page spread), and there's no dialogue or captions. *Passion of a Man* is a kind of proletarian morality play about a single woman who becomes pregnant and is kicked out of her home. Her son has to grow up on the street, and steals to get by. After being arrested for theft, he finds a blue-collar job and educates himself. He then leads a labor uprising and is arrested, tried and executed. A year later Masereel released *Mon Livre d'Heures* (*Passionate Journey*), which includes 165 sequential woodcuts and is a kind of fever dream about life in a city at the turn of the century—part *Modern Times*, part *Man with a Movie Camera*. Masereel created 58 such books throughout his career, some more narratively coherent than others. The German editions had introductions from Hermann Hesse and Thomas Mann, who wrote, "Recently, a film magazine published abroad asked me if I thought that something artistically creative could come out of the cinema. I answered: 'Indeed I do!' Then I was asked which movie, of all I had seen, had stirred me most. I replied: Masereel's *Passionate Journey*."

Masereel's work inspired other European artists, including Otto Nückel, whose worldless novel *Destiny* was made out of lead engravings and also concerns the downfall of a prole. An American wood engraver named Lynd Ward knew both Masereel and Nückel's work and, in 1929, upon seeing *Destiny*, was inspired to create his own novel in woodcuts, *Gods' Man*. The book was published

Frans Masereel,
Panels from *The Passion of a Man*, 1918

just after the stock-market crash, but still sold 20,000 copies over four years. Like *Passionate Journey*, it tells the story—with just one image per right-hand page, no text, no captions, no dialogue—of a young man vs. the city. Ward's protagonist has hypnotically wavy hair and makes a deal with a masked Mephistopheles to obtain a paintbrush that can make him a hero. The book is melodramatic and over-the-top and was later categorized as camp by Susan Sontag. After its release, it was lampooned and parodied by the cartoonist Milt Gross, who in 1930 published *He Done Her Wrong*, a wordless and illustrated (as opposed to woodcut) novel whose subtitle reads, "The Great American Novel: and not a word in it—no music, too." Ward made five more woodcut novels, his last and most complex being *Vertigo* in 1937. A few other artists contributed to the form before and after World War II: *White Collar* by Giacomo Patri, *Southern Cross* by Laurence Hyde, *The Parade* by Si Lewen. If you look at the numbers, though, the wordless novel was mostly the obsession of a pair of artists: Frans Masereel in Europe and Lynd Ward in America, with a handful of one-time-only imitators working in their wake.

N OW, AT THE risk of sounding like an asshole, I'm going to go ahead and say that "Wordless!," despite being very tasteful and sophisticated and nicely put together and well worth the price of admission, was in many ways just kind of … boring. Boring like when you go to see an orchestra play, or boring like when you're walking through an art museum. Boring because something that's been decaying and dead for quite a long time has been propped up artificially as if it were still alive.

It was less than two years before the performance of "Wordless!" at the University of Chicago that Spiegelman, on the exact same stage at the Logan Center, had warned an audience about the downside of the Faustian deal between comics and the highbrow establishment: "The danger is that it gets arid and genteel. The Faustian deal is worth making; it keeps my book in print. But it is important to have work that isn't easy to assimilate on that [academic, institutional] level." Well, "Wordless!" *was* arid and genteel. Having the jazz onstage just made it more so—jazz being an art form that for several decades was a daring and innovative and freewheeling expression of something roiling and real within the big-city American psyche, but that has now become just a fossil for tourists to take pictures of and scholars to pick apart and wonder at.

GETTING GRAPHIC

From Chicago

OUTSIDE THE BOX

Interviews with *Contemporary Cartoonists*

HILLARY L. CHUTE

"Full of fascinating, weighty insights into the artistic and working concerns of some excellent cartoonists."
—*Times Literary Supplement*

Paper $26.00

COMICS & MEDIA

A Special Issue of *Critical Inquiry*

Edited by **HILLARY L. CHUTE** and **PATRICK JAGODA**

Loaded with full-color reproductions, the essays in this book address the place of comics in both a contemporary and historical context.

The University of Chicago Press Journals
Paper $30.00

From the British Library

COMICS UNMASKED

Art and Anarchy in the UK

PAUL GRAVETT and **JOHN HARRIS DUNNING**

Gravett and Dunning have combed the British Library's extensive comic collection not only to explore the full potential of the medium but also to single out the critical points in history in which the art form challenged the status quo.

Paper $35.00

From Seagull Books

THE WASTE LAND
MARTIN ROWSON

"Irresistibly funny . . . Rowson has produced not only a first-rate comic book but also an acute critical commentary, footnotes and all. His book is a marvel of sly scholarship and invention."—*Village Voice*

Paper $17.00

The University of Chicago Press
www.press.uchicago.edu

Early on in "Wordless!," Spiegelman talked about how comics are an "in-between" medium, how they exist culturally between visual art and literature, semiotically between iconography and language, and now, socially, between entertainment and avant-gardism. This is why, he said, he likes to write the word "comics" as "co-mix"—to emphasize that comics are about mixing. That Spiegelman would bring this up and then immediately proceed to heap praise upon the wordless novel—which *doesn't* juxtapose language and images or dynamically mix stuff together in the way he claims comics are supposed to dynamically mix stuff together—just seems very odd, if not indicative of the kind of doublespeak that one would think a Mephisphelean bargain might require of a person.

In a 2004 interview with Joseph Witek, Spiegelman said, "It's that architectonics of a page that attracts me to comics, because otherwise, you really might as well go back into Lynd Ward-land and make individual compositions." The derision here in Spiegelman's voice toward Lynd Ward has something to do with what's arid, genteel and ultimately boring about the wordless novel. The compositions of Masereel, Ward and company lean too heavily on the crafted style of each picture (which surely has a lot to do with their medieval methods of carving into wood). For a comic to work really well, the prose has to be lean, the images clean. And this is what *Maus* did: the page layouts were rigorous and formal and diagrammatically dense, but the drawing style was casual-looking and unpretentious, and even though the topic at hand was almost constantly depressing, the prose was straightforward, fast-moving and frequently funny. Moreover, by borrowing the convention of the self-reflective, self-conscious comic à la *Binky Brown*, Spiegelman was able to subvert the whole thing, "passing the mic," as it were, and letting somebody else (his father) do all the talking.

This is why Spiegelman's Faustian deal with academia and the art world may bode very poorly for the future of comics. A lack of pretension, a sense of humor, a lightness of step: these are not things one associates with universities or art museums. The more you insist that comics belong there, as fodder for scholars, curators and anyone else who wants to define themselves socially by knowing how to read and patronize a difficult kind of art, the more you'll have to rewrite the history and the future of the medium so that it looks appropriately "sophisticated." It's sad to think about, but you wonder if what happened to Spiegelman in his own career—one tremendous and path-breaking success, followed by paralysis—could happen to the whole field of self-reflective, independent comics: a couple of decades of productivity, then impotence.

Here's an alternative future for comics: to do for visual iconography what Mark Twain did for English-language prose: to make it vernacular, to somehow make the look of a comic—the body language and the postures of its characters, their environment and backgrounds, the color and the lighting of the world they're in—reflect ordinary, everyday life in America. You can see this in the slumped shoulders of R. Crumb's confused and sex-obsessed hippies and burn-outs, and in the overgrown industrial detritus in the backgrounds of his panels. (His silent comic "A Short History of America" shows where all this detritus came from.) You can see it in the blank, disaffected looks of the loners and the hipsters of Dan Clowes's and Adrian Tomine's comics. And you can see it all over the place in Chris Ware's work, both in his comics and in his magazine covers (especially his Halloween cover for the *New Yorker* in 2009, where parents who are waiting on the sidewalk for their children to trick-or-treat are all looking downward at the screens of their smartphones, their faces lit up with a creepy white light like they're all wearing masks). But to emulate Twain it wouldn't be enough to just develop a visual style fit for the present. You'd have to also do what Twain did in *Huckleberry Finn* and apply that technique with irrever-ence and intensity and a fast-moving narrative to whatever it is that's killing our country like a cancer. That's the aesthetic/psychological/spiritual gauntlet that should be thrown down to comics and cartoonists—not to find their niche in the heights of the ivory tower, but to hold up a mirror to life on the ground.

SOURCES

HELL
Rob Bell, *Love Wins*
Friedrich Nietzsche, *On the Genealogy
of Morality*
Without Reservation (1989)

PUTIN AND THE WEST
Aleksandr Dugin, *The Fourth Political Theory*
Francis Fukuyama, *The End of History and the
Last Man*
Carl Schmitt, *The Concept of the Political*
William Shakespeare, *Hamlet*
Leo Tolstoy, *War and Peace*

FOES OF GOD
Don DeLillo, *Cosmopolis*
Karl Marx, *Capital*

THE EXILE'S GAME
Edward Said, "Reflections on Exile"
Calvin Tomkins, *Duchamp: A Biography*
Stefan Zweig, *Chess Story*

THE TRAGIC DIET
Paul Jaminet & Shou-Ching Jaminet,
Perfect Health Diet
Lierre Keith, *The Vegetarian Myth*
Jean-Jacques Rousseau, *Discourse on the Origin
of Inequality*
Peter Singer, *Animal Liberation*
Voltaire, *Candide*

INTO THE CAVE
Hannah Arendt, *The Human Condition*
Barbara Ehrenreich and Deirdre English,
Witches, Midwives and Nurses
Elaine Scarry, *The Body in Pain*

PRIVATE LIVES
Milovan Djilas, *Memoir of a Revolutionary*
John Stuart Mill, *On Liberty*
Jean-Jacques Rousseau, *Emile*

BEING KNOWN
Three Colors: Red (1994)
William Butler Yeats, "A Dialogue of Self
and Soul"

THE SOCIAL FILTER
The Offensive Internet, eds. Martha Nussbaum
& Saul Levmore

THE GENETIC SELF
Aldous Huxley, *Brave New World*

DISTANT READING
Ed Finn, "Becoming Yourself: The Afterlife
of Reception"
Franco Moretti, *Distant Reading
& The Bourgeois*

CONTRIBUTORS

S. G. Belknap *is a writer based in Washington, D.C. His article "Love in the Age of the Pickup Artist" appeared in Issue 2 of* The Point.

Nathaniel Comfort *is professor of the history of medicine at Johns Hopkins University. His most recent book is* The Science of Human Perfection: How Genes Became the Heart of American Medicine *(2012). He blogs at genotopia.scienceblog.com.*

Scott Esposito *is the coauthor of* The End of Oulipo? *(2013) and a senior editor for the journal of translation* Two Lines. *His essays and criticism have appeared in the* Washington Post, *the* Times Literary Supplement, *and the* White Review.

Dawn Herrera-Helphand *is a doctoral candidate in the University of Chicago's Committee on Social Thought.*

Rob Horning *is an editor of the* New Inquiry.

Ben Jeffery *is a Ph.D. student in the University of Chicago's Committee on Social Thought. His essay for Issue 2 of* The Point *"Hard Feelings" was later expanded into a book entitled* Anti-Matter: Michel Houellebecq and Depressive Realism *(2011). His most recent* Point *essay was "Out with the New," which appeared in Issue 6.*

Brickey LeQuire *is a lecturer in Political Science at Samford University. His essay "Not Even Past" appeared in Issue 5 of* The Point.

Jesse McCarthy *is a graduate student in English at Princeton University. His dissertation examines African American novels through the lens of modernist aesthetics and Cold War cultural politics in mid-century America. His article "Who Will Pay Reparations on My Soul?" appeared on* The Point's *website this summer.*

Thomas Meaney *is a doctoral candidate in History at Columbia. He has written for the* New York Review of Books, *the* London Review of Books *and the* Times Literary Supplement.

Meghan O'Gieblyn *is a writer based in Madison, Wisconsin. Her work has appeared most recently in the* Oxford American, Guernica *and* Indiana Review.

Tim Peters *writes from Urbana, Illinois. His work has appeared in the* Review of Contemporary Fiction, *the* Los Angeles Review of Books *and the* Rumpus. *His article "Chris Ware's ANL #20" appeared in Issue 4 of* The Point.

Steven Poole *is the author of* Unspeak *(2007) and* Trigger Happy: Video Games and the Entertainment Revolution *(2004). He lives in London.*

Lowry Pressly *is a Ph.D. candidate in political theory at Harvard University. His fiction and criticism have appeared in the* Los Angeles Review of Books, Jurist *and the* Yale Journal of International Law.

Thomas Chatterton Williams *is the author of the memoir* Losing My Cool: Love, Literature and a Black Man's Escape from the Crowd *(2011). His writing has appeared in the* New York Times, *the* Wall Street Journal, *the* Washington Post *and the* Atlantic. *He currently lives in Paris, where he is at work on a screenplay and a novel.*

THE POINT

COMING IN ISSUE TEN:

ISIS and the dream of the Caliphate

•

What are drugs for?

•

Philosophy and gossip

•

Leonard Cohen: Artist or saint?

SUBSCRIBE AT
WWW.THEPOINTMAG.COM

$18 FOR ONE YEAR (2 ISSUES)
$32 FOR TWO YEARS (4 ISSUES)

BACK ISSUES AVAILABLE

LOVE IN THE AGE OF THE PICKUP ARTIST	THE CONSOLATIONS OF SELF-HELP	HARD FEELINGS	PREDATORY HABITS
"i first turned to the pickup artists after losing in love"	"it was my life coach who first introduced me to eckhart tolle"	"michel houellebecq has published four novels, all of them bitter and miserable"	"amidst nature's unreasonable scarcity, wall street often seems like a refuge of reason"